禅生活

# living zen

## michael paul

ABBEVILLE PRESS

new york   london   paris

**For Kumiko-san, whose love and compassion has shown me the way.**

First published in the United States of America by Abbeville Press in 2000.

First published in Great Britain by Frances Lincoln Limited 2000.

First edition

10 9 8 7 6 5 4 3 2 1

*Library of Congress Cataloging-in-Publication Data*

Paul, Michael, 1945-
    Living Zen/Michael Paul; shodo by Yoko Murata.
       p. cm.
    Includes index.
    ISBN 0-7892-0681-1
      1. Zen Buddhism. I. Murata, Yoko.

    BQ9265.4 .P38 2000
    294.3'927--dc21

Project editors: Cathy Fischgrund and Ginny Surtees
Editor: James Harpur
Designer: Sarah Slack
Production: Hazel Kirkman
Indexer: Marie Lorimer
Proofreader: Judith Warren

# contents

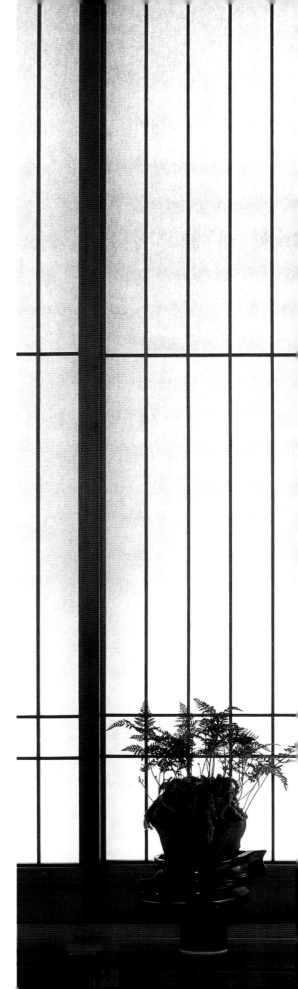

# an affirmation of life

Living Zen introduces us to the simplicity, naturalness and depth of beauty found in Zen Buddhism. It is an invitation to look at life afresh, from the perspective of this profound spiritual tradition.

Living Zen has only one aim: to encourage us to take a longer and closer look at all that is around us in the hope that once we have developed a more intense insight we will grow to cherish and nurture this earth and its inhabitants. By living Zen we learn to acquire a heightened awareness. For Zen sharpens our senses and intensifies our powers of perception and so enriches all our experiences. Even everyday events take on a new meaning. The ordinary is transformed into the extraordinary; the extraordinary becomes an everyday experience.

Be alive,
be here – and know
the beat of your heart

To achieve this insight we first have to understand more about ourselves. When we practise Zen we embark on an inner journey of self-discovery – a journey that leads to a deeper understanding not only of our minds but also of our concept of reality. Through Zen meditation we eventually learn to penetrate the core of our existence so that finally we can see the true nature of our inner selves and the things around us.

Zen teaches us how to become free of the deceptions of the mind and to recognize the full potential of our lives. It is only when we achieve this clarity that we make the breakthrough and realize one of Zen's amazing truths: that how we see ourselves is how we see the universe. For Zen leads us to the ultimate realization that our own human life force and the life force of everything in the universe – whether it is a planet, a mountain, a river, a tree, a plant, a person, an animal, a fish or an insect – are one and the same.

For many of us today, Western philosophy seems incapable of explaining the real meaning of life or of fully satisfying our deepest spiritual desires. But Zen, with its

original perspective, shows that if we really want to penetrate the inner truth we must become free of the life-long conditioning and preconceptions that have restricted and shackled our minds.

In the Western world we have learned to look at things in a way that we regard as logical. We believe that everything in existence has a twofold nature, which we divide into categories such as mental and physical or good and evil. However, this doctrine of dualism on which our logic, philosophies and religions are based does not exist in Zen. What is more, if we examine Zen with a dualistic mentality we will find it confusing and irrational. That is because it is not logical – if anything, it is the antithesis of the dualistic way of thinking. Western logic teaches us to call black black and white white. But Zen refutes this rigid adherence to reasoning. This is not to say that Zen is contrary to common sense; nor is it beyond comprehension. It simply offers us a new, more intuitive understanding of the way we live our lives – free from a dichotomous approach of logic and from the separation of the "self."

This perception of a new reality leads to Zen's precious gift of freedom – freedom from delusions of the ego and from opinion and prejudice. Above all it gives us freedom of the spirit and mind. Zen wants our thoughts to be clear and unobstructed in everything we do, so we can open ourselves to the full extent of its profundity.

It is for this reason that in Zen practice there are no parameters. No limits, cardinal doctrines or philosophies are imposed on the mind. Zen is free of religious dogma and sacred tenets that limit our thinking or inhibit our actions. However, it is not the aim of Zen to undermine established beliefs or challenge traditional religious teachings. All it asks is that we live our lives with compassion, creativity and a deep respect for all living things.

When we trace the history of Zen back to its beginnings, we can see its close connection with nature. The Buddha's teachings that we should respect all life, the naturalistic ideals of Taoism, which shaped Chinese Zen (Ch'an), and the

appreciation of the Japanese for the natural world all combined to give Zen its essential affinity with nature. From the outset, Zen scholars recognized that nature and human creativity were synonymous. The two were considered part of the natural order of the universe – and it was through nature's intense images that many Zen-inspired artists sought to express its living energy, inspiration and wisdom. For in Zen, art that depicts nature is considered an affirmation of life.

The Zen masters understood that nature lives in us and that we live in nature. For them nature was the "greatest cathedral," and they strove through their work to open our eyes to the magnificence of the universe so we would revere and respect it for all time. In this age of environmental destruction, this book, in its own small way, endeavors to continue the mission of these ancient artists by encouraging a greater understanding of Zen's asceticism and by advocating its innate relationship with nature.

Through my photographs on the following pages I have attempted to see beneath the surface in order to capture the "spirit of Zen" and illustrate its sometimes elusive and abstract nature. These images are designed to go straight to the centre of the object to reveal its inner beauty and truth. Through my words I have tried to explain, in the simplest terms, the essence of Zen and its fundamental convictions. But be aware that this is not intended as a definitive work on this subject. There is a wealth of literature that can explain more fully its intimate workings and wisdom. And above all, in your search for enlightenment, keep in mind the Zen axiom that the real truth can often be written about but never properly expressed. Instead, it must be directly experienced.

It is therefore my hope that when you open this book you will also open your mind. For it is my deepest wish that the images and words in this book inspire you to take a look at the world from a different viewpoint and in time you will discover the riches and rewards of living Zen.

# understanding
# zen

Soft light
through shoji –
blood red rosehips

# birth

Much of what is known about Zen Buddhism in the Western world today has come from Japan, although its origins can be traced back to the India of some 2,500 years ago and the birth of Buddhism. Yet if the seeds of Zen were originally sown in India, it was in China that it really took root. From China Zen spread to Korea in the fourth century CE, finally reaching Japan in the twelfth century.

Buddha mind –
unlock
the treasury of truth

According to Buddhist tradition, Siddhartha Gautama, the man who became known as the Buddha – which means "Awakened One" – was born in northern India in 563 B.C.E. His father is believed to have been a wealthy maharaja, or king, of the Shakya tribe; and later in life the Buddha became known as Shakyamuni – "wise man of the Shakya tribe." In his early life as a prince, Siddhartha Gautama was shielded from the suffering and pain of the world that surrounded him. But eventually, after four profound and life-changing encounters with the grim reality of the outside world, he left the palace, renouncing the privileged and luxurious life of his father's court. He became a wandering mendicant and set out on his long spiritual journey in search of the truth.

After many years of searching, his awakening came after an extended period of meditation under a banyan tree, later known as the Bodhi ("Enlightenment") tree. Early one morning as he saw the morning star rise, a great clarity and insight came over him – as though he was seeing the star for the first and only time. He was able to see it without separation or subjective interpretation: he became that star and the vast space of the universe. It was then, at that instant, that Siddhartha Gautama became the Buddha and that the Buddhist faith was born.

From the wisdom found in his enlightenment, the Buddha formulated his teachings that, although intensively practical, were filled with compassion and hope in order to show others the way beyond the suffering and burdens of everyday life. Revered by his disciples and followers, he traveled around India for many years, attracting vast crowds with his profound words.

Red leaves

up temple steps

start this spiritual journey

It was during one of these gatherings that the first "Zen encounter" is said to have occurred. One day, in front of a large crowd on Vulture Peak Mountain in northern India, the Buddha, instead of giving a discourse, simply held up a lotus flower without saying a word. All the onlookers stared at him with incomprehension – except one disciple, Kashyapa, who broke into a smile. For he alone had understood the Buddha's action: that it was a transmission of the truth, or *dharma* – a teaching without words, from mind to mind, from heart to heart.

This transmission of truth "beyond words" was passed down through the centuries from master to disciple and is still recognized as one of the fundamental methods of Zen teaching. However, in Zen, the word translated into English as "transmission" literally means "being at one" – that is, being in spiritual harmony with one another. Consequently the term implies more a shared experience between teacher and student than the direct transference of the truth. For the Buddha stressed that the truth cannot simply be handed down from person to person. Instead, we must all find the truth for ourselves, inside our hearts.

Although Buddhism was probably established in China as early as the first century c.e., the original form of Zen, known as Ch'an, did not begin to take root as a separate school of thought until the fifth century. The man who brought this about was the great Indian Buddhist missionary Bodhidharma, who is ranked as the twenty-eighth Indian patriarch after the Buddha and the first Chinese Buddhist patriarch. It was through Bodhidharma's ideas and his more radical approach to teaching that a new style of Buddhism developed. Over the next few centuries Bodhidharma's beliefs became assimilated with Chinese philosophy, and various Taoist scholars added their own interpretations and adapted the basic tenets of Buddhism to suit the more pragmatic characteristics of China's own ancient culture. Hence Ch'an, prior to its final transformation to Japanese Zen, became a blend of the spiritual traditions of Indian Buddhism and Chinese Taoism and Confucianism.

Many myths and legends surround this first ancestor of Zen, the majority of them disputed by modern Zen scholars. Nevertheless, Bodhidharma is still credited with the well-known verse that is often used to describe the meaning of Zen:

*A special transmission outside of the scriptures.*
*No dependence on words or letters*
*Seeing directly into the human mind*
*Realizing our true nature, becoming Buddha.*

Although Buddhism itself had been recognized in Japan since the sixth century c.e., Zen itself, as a distinct belief system, did not become established until the twelfth century. This came about largely through the efforts of two monks, Eisai and his disciple Dogen, who are credited as the first Japanese to travel to China to bring back Zen practice to Japan. In time these two important Zen patriarchs were to establish, respectively, the Rinzai and Soto sects – the two principal Zen schools in Japan today. The teachings of the two men are still revered and Dogen's major work, *The Shobogenzo*, is considered to be one of the most important Buddhist texts.

Until its arrival in Japan, Zen Buddhism had mainly been shaped by Chinese Taoism. Many aspects of Indian Buddhism – particularly the mystical and metaphysical parts – did not appeal to the very practical Chinese. So the Taoists simply adapted Buddhist ideology to suit the characteristics and culture of the Chinese people. In essence Zen is Chinese. However, it was the Japanese who added to Zen arguably its most vital ingredient: simplicity. The Japanese understanding of beauty and worth has always been based on the simple things in life and they have always honoured and respected the spirit and power of nature. So when Zen was introduced from China with its sage-like wisdom and Taoist images of the natural world woven into its language and art forms, it complemented the already existing Japanese sense of aesthetics. And when they had absorbed Zen to the very core of their being, Zen's Japanese followers expressed it with even greater refinement and focus.

As Zen blossomed in Japan it instigated a new period of artistic achievement and intellectual ferment. Poets, painters, architects, gardeners and scholars all discovered in Zen a philosophy that affirmed their judgments and provided a deeper meaning to their work. The warrior class, aristocrats and common people also found it completely compatible. In short, Zen could not have suited the Japanese psyche better and so it flourished with a new energy and purpose.

It was not until the beginning of the twentieth century that Zen's rich spiritual culture began to pervade the Western world. The man who was perhaps the most forceful in spreading this Asian belief system beyond Southeast Asia was Daisetz T. Suzuki, a Buddhist of the Rinzai school. Suzuki's mastery of the English language and his marriage to an American woman gave him an insight into Anglo-American culture not previously shared by other Zen teachers. This gave him the depth of understanding needed to bridge the two hemispheres and find his way into the hearts and minds of Western philosophers and thinkers. Suzuki's pioneering work outside Japan was significant and has made a profound impact on the way Zen has been practiced in the West.

As Zen tradition underwent a transformation in the West it grew in appeal as a result of its mysticism and opposition to conventional and rational thought. Its popularity soon encouraged many Westerners to journey to Japan and likewise many Japanese Zen masters to visit the West to meet the increasing demand for veritable instruction. The transition from one culture to another undoubtedly propagated many modifications to Zen's core traditions, and many new schools and secularized forms were established.

Today there are Zen Buddhist monasteries, retreats and centers throughout America and Europe. Zen has filtered down to all levels of society and has influenced the art forms, architecture, language and culture of contemporary life. It remains an influential spiritual force that continues to gain momentum throughout the modern world.

# meaning

The spread of Buddhism in Southeast Asia gave rise to the Japanese and consequently the Western versions of Zen that we know today. Zen's ideas did not evolve from a single source but were born from a confluence of many different Asian cultures and belief systems. Scholars today consider Zen to be a crystallization of all the essential Far Eastern philosophies and disciplines, resulting in a highly practical approach to everyday life.

Zen is a Japanese word that derives from the Chinese word *chan*. This in turn originally came from the Indian Sanskrit word *dhyana,* which can be translated as "meditation" – but it can also refer to a state of mind or practice that goes beyond subject and object.

At the outset, the meaning of Zen can be a difficult concept to grasp. This is because Zen is an experience or a way of life – not a belief. A closer understanding shows it to be a totally abstract thought process, not based on logic or analysis. Unlike Western religions or philosophies, Zen has no sacred books, cardinal doctrines or dogmatic tenets that are imposed on its followers. Zen adopts a totally passive position. It relies on us to teach ourselves. Zen merely points the way and through its insight it opens our minds to make them more receptive to its spiritual riches and ineffably deep experiences.

It has often been said by Zen masters and scholars that Zen is so elusive as an idea that it cannot be explained in words. Yet for many people it is its sheer simplicity that is most appealing. At its most basic level Zen is a state of pure sentient awareness that allows us to look at life from a fresh perspective – a new vantage point. One of the ways it does this is by helping us to understand our true nature through the process of self-realization and by exposing our self-imposed illusions. Zen is the road to self-discovery. It leads us to the truth inside ourselves: for once we understand ourselves we also understand what it is like to experience our true "Buddha-nature."

Mountain temple –
faint sound of a bell
ringing in the mist

People in the West from all walks of life have turned to Zen for the insight and clarity it provides for everyday living. Zen is about letting go – being free from all that stands in the way of our true potential. When it comes to self-expression Zen has no fixed limits. Over the years it has inspired artists, writers and poets as well as helping countless individuals find a more productive approach to their lives.

Zen is not a religion in the way we understand the meaning in the West. In Zen there is no God to worship, but at the same time it does not dispute or affirm the existence of one. It is not preoccupied with pious deeds, ceremonial rites or prayers of devotion. Nor does Zen concern itself with saving souls or the immortality of others, or hold out the inducements of heaven or the intimidation of hell. This, however, should not be interpreted to mean that Zen lacks a clear set of ethics or a code of behavior or that it supports irreverence or immorality.

As will be seen, Zen with its Buddhist foundations is highly moral and principled. Zen teaches us to act with wisdom and compassion. Today there are many believers from other religions who practise Zen along with their own faiths. It simply wants to rise above all conventional convictions and to seek a higher affirmation of reality free from religious encumbrances.

Without doubt the fundamental precepts of Zen were born from Buddhism; nevertheless its directness and simplicity stand in sharp contrast to the metaphysical abstractions and complex rites of other Buddhist sects. Among many schools of modern Zen thought, its relationship with everyday life and its emphasis on personal experience have served to separate it almost entirely from its religious connections and from the Indian mysticism that still permeates Mahayana and Theravada Buddhist practice. Perhaps the greatest difference between Zen and other forms of Buddhism is its sense of spiritual freedom. Zen has deliberately denounced its own teachings, burned its books, smashed its idols and statues – even refused to call itself by its given name. Zen is almost like a religion without religious limitations or strictures.

# teachings

Since Zen claims to be neither a religion nor a philosophy it imposes few beliefs or sacred tenets on its followers. Zen argues that beliefs often distort reality and tend to stop us from seeing the truth clearly within ourselves. For this reason Zen has no specific code of conduct: you are responsible for your own actions. Zen does not condemn, nor does it tell you what to do. It has complete faith in our inner purity and goodness, and it trusts each individual to discover the truth. All Zen does is point the way through its practical teachings and the clarity and insight it can provide. Its methods of teaching and awakening the mind stem largely from its Japanese, Indian Buddhist and Chinese Taoist traditions, which have been refined over many thousands of years.

Zen spirit –
an insatiable seeker
of truth

*Meditation*: In Zen, meditation involves sitting quietly in contemplation. It is the method by which you can go into your mind and discover what lies within, allowing you to witness your inner soul and consciousness. Training and refining the technique helps us to strip away all the delusions and layers of conditioning caused by the habit of dualistic thought – often referred to in Zen as "the dust on the mirror of our soul." Although many religions and philosophies use meditation as part of their practice, Zen has developed a unique form of it through the technique of studying *koans*.

*Koans*: These are anecdotes or stories about the lives or the teachings of Zen patriarchs and often deal with exchanges between master and student. In Zen training they are used as vehicles for spiritual enlightenment and are studied during meditation and long periods of contemplation. Their role is to help students train their minds and induce enlightenment. *Koans* are one of Zen's methods of "direct pointing." By provoking introspection, they point to the nature of ultimate reality and contain a wealth of insight into the morality and the ethics of Zen. *Koans* are deliberately designed to have an apparently cryptic or paradoxical content in order to steer the student away from seeking rational solutions. There are many different collections of *koans* that have evolved

over the centuries, the more notable works being Hekiganroku's *The Blue Cliff Record* and Mumonkan's much quoted publication *The Gateless Gate*.

*Zen practice*: Liturgy, rituals and services of worship differ from one Zen center to another. Because Zen practice in the East is still largely monastic, the whole focus of life centers on meditation and experiences that lead to awakening. Conversely, for lay practitioners in the West, who tend to have a more complex, demanding lifestyle, the practice of Zen usually comes down to the individual and how much he or she wants to be committed to the discipline and way of life. In reality for all Zen students there is a lot of hard work involved in reaching spiritual enlightenment. On occasions, intense periods of meditation called *sesshin* are held at most Zen centers, followed by *koan* practice, work periods and exchanges between student and teacher. There are also sessions of chanting often before meals or at the close of the day's activities. Outside the temple, lay Zen students usually have a daily routine of meditation, while some develop their own liturgy at home, which may involve incense, chanting and setting up a small altar.

*Vows and precepts*: In formal Zen Buddhist practice, monks and nuns, as well as lay practitioners, undertake to be true to a set of four vows (see below) that originate from Buddhist beliefs. These vows essentially affirm the desire for awakening, but they vary according to the school. Students chant them three times, with full awareness of their implications, then prostrate themselves in front of the image of Buddha:

> *All beings without number,*
> *I vow to liberate.*
> *Endless blind passions,*
> *I vow to uproot*
> dharma *gates without number,*
> *I vow to penetrate.*
> *The great way of Buddha,*
> *I vow to attain.*

Many practicing Zen Buddhists also adopt ten precepts that are not dissimilar to the Ten Commandments in Judaism and Christianity. These are: "Not to kill; not to steal; not to engage in sexual misconduct; not to lie; not to become intoxicated; not to criticize the faults of others; not to be proud; not to covet; not to give way to anger; not to malign the three treasures – the Buddha, the teaching and the Buddhist Community."

Despite the lack of an established doctrine, Zen is highly principled. Its self-imposed precepts are based on avoidance of anything that causes detriment, suffering or delusion to either oneself or others. Zen followers make a clear commitment to refrain from harming all living beings and exercise a deep love and respect for all life. This compassion does not discriminate between different races, species or religions.

Zen followers also revere the vows of the Buddha – "the Bodhisattva of Compassion" – to care for others and to save all beings. The Buddha, who devoted his life for the sake of enlightenment and to helping others achieve it for themselves, practised the six *paramitas*, or virtues, of generosity, ethics, patience, effort, meditation, and wisdom. These are taught in some schools of Zen.

Zen also encourages a deep affection for the environment and the natural world. This is because Zen recognizes the unity of the human race with the universe and the role we play in nature's cycle of life and death. Zen Buddhists tend to eat vegetarian food, abstain from taking drugs and refrain from using things that harm the natural environment.

Because Zen emphasizes compassion and wisdom, a great many Zen practitioners involve themselves in charities and community activities. Zen centers of all nations are often committed to promoting world peace and understanding, while many carry out important work in the community, caring for sick, dying or distressed people.

Leaves like fire

float down

to meet green water

# enlightenment

The experience of enlightenment is the culmination of all Zen achievement. Since the day the Buddha attained his awakening under the Bodhi tree, practicing Buddhists regard enlightenment as the quintessential human experience.

Called *kensho* or *satori* in Japanese, enlightenment is the means in Zen of attaining the "inner truth" – to gain a new viewpoint on life that allows us to surpass the superficiality of the world and discover the truth hidden within our inner selves. For Zen monks, nuns and even committed lay followers it is the key that opens the door to the true life of Zen and the pinnacle of their training – since all their discipline and efforts have been directed towards its attainment. For them it is the awakening of a new sense and represents both a new beginning and the final destination.

*Kensho*, which means "the vision of the self" or "the essence," arises from a sudden, profound inner perception that strikes at the very root of our existence. In conventional religious terms *kensho* could be categorized as a mystical phenomenon. But as with many things in Zen, it is an experience that has attracted many abstract definitions. Many great Zen masters and modern Zen writers and theologians have tried to explain *kensho* – but like other profound spiritual states it can only be experienced personally and defies accurate description. Nevertheless, in modern-day Zen it has come to mean directly experiencing one's true nature – the crossing over to a farther shore and a world previously hidden by the mists of delusions created by our dualistic minds.

It should be emphasized that Zen enlightenment can only be reached by ourselves: nobody else can do it for us. All Zen can do, even by way of the greatest Zen teachers, is to direct and point us along the way so that we can focus all our attention on attaining this ultimate Zen experience. For Zen insists that *kensho* must grow out of ourselves; otherwise the experience and wisdom it brings are not ours but just borrowed plumage.

The late Daisetz Suzuki, in his seminal work *An Introduction to Zen Buddhism*, claimed that "*satori* is the *raison d'être* of Zen." Without it, he asserted, "there is no Zen." This may be true within the confines of formal, monastic life in which devoted Zen followers make the attainment of *satori* the overriding purpose of all their efforts. However, modern Zen scholars argue that too much emphasis can be placed on the attainment of this state of mind and that despite its exalted status it is not an essential achievement for practicing everyday Zen. For many it is the journey, the path that is trodden on the way to enlightenment rather than the ultimate destination, that is the most important. The training and practice and the inner strength and composure gained from meditation are the great gifts that Zen bestows on its followers and which bring fulfilment in themselves.

When, where and how does enlightenment occur? Contrary, perhaps, to popular myth, it does not happen at the top of the highest mountain peak at the break of dawn, or at the moment when the orchestra swells to a crescendo. More often it is triggered by an insignificant incident or unconscious action. It does not come at a particular time or in a special place but usually creeps up on us when we least expect it. For many devoted Zen followers it happens after many hours of practising *zazen*, or sitting in meditation – often following extended periods of *koan* study when the rational mind has exhausted all possibilities and has found no solution. But when the breakthrough does come it is unmistakable. It is as if bells ring and lights come on in your mind – and, in a flash of consciousness, you discover your real self. Zen, however, insists that this new perception of reality has actually been lying dormant inside you all along but that all this time you had kept your mind closed to its great truth.

The ancient Indian method of systematically opening the mind to achieve this higher level of consciousness has traditionally been through meditation. The Sanskrit word for meditation, *dhyana*, denotes three states of mind: concentration, meditation and contemplation. And in Buddhism it is the combination of these three faculties that leads to the moment of awakening. In Zen itself, the role of meditation – which is explained in more depth in the next chapter – principally concerns itself with the awakening of the mind so that we can see into our inner world. It is a tried-and-tested Zen Buddhist discipline designed to lead us to the truth about ourselves. Although meditation is a vehicle that leads to enlightenment, the two are not necessarily linked inextricably and one can exist without the other.

Essentially the practice of Zen meditation teaches us to be in pure attentiveness prior to the realization of the internal mystery. It prepares the mind for what is to come – for enlightenment is almost entirely an inner occurrence, a truly personal experience that helps us to understand our original being, known as "One Mind" in Buddhism. As a famous Zen master remarked, "Enlightenment is about seeing through one's own essential nature. When this remarkable insight happens, one sees the essential nature of the universe . . . the true meaning of reality." This profound experience is referred to as seeing the 'inner truth' in Zen Buddhism or one's "Buddha-nature."

At this point it is probably worth dispelling another myth about Zen. Enlightenment is not, as some people may believe, a hazy spiritual trance or dreamlike abstraction. In fact, *kensho* or *satori* is a perfectly normal state of mind that is only evident by the composure, sense of peace and deep happiness that its recipient radiates. Zen proclaims that enlightenment is nothing special and insists that in this state you continue to behave as an ordinary human being who has not risen above others. However, with enlightenment comes a pure awareness rarely experienced. It is as if all our faculties become tuned to a higher key. Transformed at a deep level, we see everything around us with clarity and understanding. The world takes on a different intensity: flowers look more beautiful, the birds sing more sweetly, the sky seems bluer. For Zen has delivered the greatest rewards of life: joy, peace and deep satisfaction.

## awareness

Once when he was asked what Zen was, a great master replied, "Attention. Attention. Attention." What he meant was that Zen requires total concentration. This is because Zen wants us to pay full attention to the smallest details in life – to be mindful of everything we do. For Zen recognizes that true awareness transforms every aspect of our lives down to the most basic of experiences.

Wise practitioners of Zen are not sidetracked by its Buddhist metaphysical abstractions or its mystical subtleties. Instead, they immerse themselves in the events of everyday experiences. This emphasis on everyday living teaches us to become fully aware of our actions as well as their consequences. Furthermore, it is often said that Zen transforms the ordinary into the extraordinary: so whatever our actions – whether cleaning the house, washing the car, walking the dog or weeding the garden – Zen gives us a sense of purpose by making sure we perform them for their own sake with all our attention and commitment.

One of Zen's best known maxims comes from a Chinese poet:

> How wondrous, how miraculous.
> I draw water, I chop wood.

This type of focused awareness in Zen transforms our ability to see from a different vantage point. While Zen enlightenment helps us see life from a fresh perspective and brings about a remarkable realization of the truth, enlightenment in itself is not essential to awaken our senses. Every aspect of Zen's practical everyday training improves our powers of perception so that people, places, objects and events can all be seen with a new clarity and purpose.

Novices to Zen are curious as to what exactly Zen lets us see. Normally, when we observe an object from a philosophical perspective, we remain on the outside, observing only what is there. But Zen teaches us to transcend the outer world and

White water lily

still pure

when storms subside

cut right through to the inner essence. It is like seeing something or someone for the very first time. Zen's way of looking at an object, image or person is experiential – it does not compare, disparage or discriminate. Through the insight Zen brings we learn to see the very spirit of the object – not just the form. Ultimately the subject becomes the object, the musician becomes the music, the singer becomes the song. Zen encourages us not to separate ourselves from the object we are seeing. Instead, we must close the gap; break down the barriers; let go of all that appears rational and familiar and see things afresh. Zen tells us to try to become one with the object of our perception and not to remain an outside observer. Just as the Buddha became the morning star and saw it without the separation of the self, we must learn to see things as they really are.

Above all, Zen teaches us to see right into the intimate nature of the object without the hindrance of conventional judgments or a preconditioned mind. It does this by making us let go of the self, which is responsible for our concept of separateness. The problem is that in our present state we are so programmed to evaluate things from this perspective that we cannot see what we are looking at. It is a dilemma well encapsulated by John Daido Loori, the eminent abbot of Zen Mountain Monastery in Mt. Tremper, New York, who says in his classic work *Mountain Record of Zen Talks*:

"The fact is that when we look at something, whether it's an object in nature, a photographic subject or a created image we are so programmed that we really cannot see what we are looking at. Even if it is something we have never seen before our internal reference system goes to work fitting what we see into a slot that we are familiar with. Once we have that familiar category we plug into a whole reference system of the associations, feelings, information, and preconceived judgments that make up our life-long experience. We are conditioned to see in a certain way. What that conditioning does is protect and strengthen the idea of a separate self that we have been building layer by layer since infancy. We cannot see – see things as if for the first time, see things as they really are – until we let go of the separate self."

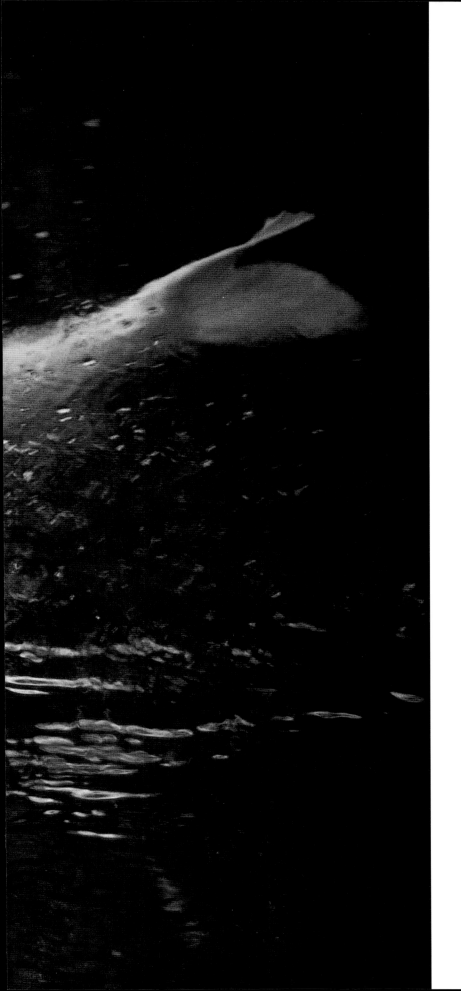

## living zen
## every day

Golden carp –
sunlight in the water
icy mountain stream

# practical zen

Living Zen is not an escape from everyday life, nor is it spent in isolation from the real world. Nor is it, as some may imagine, an elusive Eastern abstraction that transcends the actualities of living, involving only the aesthetic in the pursuit of profound spiritual experiences. Without question, Zen is not a cult religion or a weird sect with strange rituals. Zen neither threatens society nor preaches anarchy. Moreover, in contrast to the classical Zen training of Japan or China, lay Zen practitioners today are not required to shave their heads or wear robes or sandals – for Zen was not specifically created for monks or nuns in far-removed retreats. Instead, Zen is for everyone to practice every day: a practical, down-to-earth approach to living designed for ordinary people leading ordinary lives.

It must be stressed that living Zen every day is not easy. If it no longer demands rigorous spiritual training or monastic hardships, it nevertheless does require self-discipline, perseverance and great tenacity. It also requires proper instruction and astute guidance. The importance of a good teacher cannot be underestimated. However, when we strip away the surface formality, mysticism and liturgy of classical Zen training and get down to its essence we discover that Zen is the perfect way to live our everyday lives. In fact Zen is simply life itself. It involves every aspect of our daily lives, from work and play to emotional relationships and bringing up children.

Zen was designed to deal with the everyday realities of life. Stemming from its earliest Chinese origins, Zen was shaped as a practical approach to living life to the fullest. The wealth of Zen literature, including *koans* and the ancient wisdom of the patriarchs and masters, are often considered "dead" teachings or mere intellectualizing compared with the immediacy of applying Zen everyday. There is a saying in Zen that we should "examine the living words, not the dead ones" – meaning that we should concern ourselves only with those things that have practical relevance and ignore those concepts that cease to contribute to life's everyday experiences.

What really matters is that Zen deals with the present. It teaches us that this life is too precious to waste. Zen is about the joy of living right now – a celebration of everyday life as it happens. There is an immediacy about Zen that encourages us to live for the moment. Zen students are forever being exhorted by their masters to "wake up!" – to bring the mind back to the present; to be here – *now*; to look for the depth of the moment rather than for permanency; to be aware of every aspect of life.

Stripped of all its trappings, Zen is about enjoying the simple things. It promotes a lightness to life, a sense of calm, an eye for beauty, a song in the heart. And this is what makes it so appealing. Zen's spontaneity and freedom transforms everyday events into the extraordinary. Things we once took for granted now take on a new meaning, and routine chores become life's little pleasures.

This should not be construed to mean that Zen enables us to lead our lives in a continuous altered state of consciousness or as if we were always "on a high." On the contrary, Zen brings us right down to earth and insists that we live as "normal" human beings. Zen's practicalities provide common sense and clarity, allowing us to live sane and satisfied lives by instilling us with a serene and patient attitude to life's vagaries.

Zen is often portrayed as being "nothing special." But it is not as simple as that. It is more that Zen makes everything special and so no one thing stands out as being more special than any other. On one occasion during the days of the Chinese Tang dynasty (618–907 C.E.), a Taoist master, when asked to explain Taoism, replied, "When you are hungry, you eat; when you are thirsty, you drink." Zen embraces this same simplicity, recognizing that its own meaning is deeply embedded in the subconsciousness of our everyday actions.

Zen's practical approach to life can be traced back to its Taoist influences. The Chinese have always been considered to be practical people by nature. So while the Chinese scholars and thinkers who shaped the ideology of Zen were inspired by

Indian Buddhist beliefs, they never let go of the practical side of life inherent in their own culture, and adapted the teachings of Buddhism accordingly. They discarded the more speculative teachings and the other elements at odds with their native pragmatism, such as the metaphysical aspects of Buddhism, while retaining Buddhism's more profound ideas and penetrating analysis. This adaptation to the Chinese culture essentially transformed Indian Buddhism into Zen Buddhism.

One of the unique features of the first Zen monasteries in China – whose tradition has lasted to this day – was their newfound principle of complete democracy. This distinguished them from the more exclusive *sangha* or brotherhood of Indian Buddhism and meant that everyone, including the master and elders, became equally involved in the manual labor and menial tasks required in the day-to-day running of the monastery. This emphasis on ordinary activities in Zen monasteries and retreats still exists today. Through Zen we discover that if we approach everyday tasks in the right way they can become a form of meditation and connect the outer world of objects with the inner world of consciousness. Zen teaches us to find satisfaction and reward in everything we do and makes no distinction between drawing water and chopping wood, even after enlightenment; Zen transforms these menial tasks into life's rewarding rituals.

Another aspect of early Zen monastic life that also emphasized life's practicalities was its detachment from words, canonical books and even sacred Buddhist *sutras*, or writings. While Christian monks and Buddhist monks of other schools led reclusive lives of prayer and immersed themselves in study, penance and other pious activities, Zen monks adopted an altogether more practical approach to learning, witnessed in the short and cryptic early sermons and teaching methods of the Zen masters. These in turn stimulated questions and debate, often resulting in answers that were both ambiguous and obscure. And these required resolution by direct action and intellectual ingenuity rather than by a traditional reliance on learning by rote.

Pure thought
like honey
collected by bees

## self-discovery

Living Zen is a process of self-discovery and each day of our lives involves one more step along this road to a deeper insight into our own true nature. One of Zen's more subjective endeavors is to help us to investigate our minds exhaustively and in so doing provide an insight into our inner world. Going beyond all material concepts that we have of the "self," Zen seeks to unmask our "original face" so we can see who we really are and get in touch with the "eye of the soul" – the hidden truth that lies within us all.

How do we access this hidden truth? In our normal state of consciousness governed by a dualistic state of being, our thoughts are conditioned to conceal the identity of our true self from our conscious ego. From years of "mind programming," all of us have barriers to the truth in the form of long-established opinions or prejudices. Consequently, whenever we experience anything, these preprogrammed judgments are automatically triggered and more often than not delude the mind by hiding the real truth. In Zen, however, meditation enables us to avoid the pitfalls of these self-imposed illusions. Using Zen's oblique approach of "single-pointedness" we can slip past these mental obstacles and experience our true "Buddha-nature."

Our Buddha-nature simply means the real self – that is, the true or original nature of what we really are. We discover our Buddha-nature when the mind becomes at one with the mind of the Buddha – an identification by which ultimate truth is transmitted to us. When this happens we achieve enlightenment – we cross over to the farther shore, experience the awakening to the true self and identify all reality with our Buddha-nature. As the Zen master Dogen once taught, "To study the way of the Buddha is to study the self, and to study the self is to forget the self; to forget the self is to be enlightened by all things."

When we reach this state of true self-realization a whole new inner world opens up. By discovering our own true nature, we free ourselves from the things that inhibited our full potential. Like a flower opening in the sunshine, we begin to realize the

brilliant light of our creativity and capacity for achievement. In our previous state, restricted by our opinions and preconceptions, many of us might have believed that we had gone as far as we could go. But once we have cast off the shackles that imprisoned our minds, we find there is no limit to our talents and ability and we are ready to try every new experience and open ourselves to a whole new world. With its strong belief in self-expression, Zen is by its very nature a catalyst for creative thought – its spiritual freedom allows us to discover our creative powers and hidden potential. By exploring our creativity, we develop a greater sense of self-realization. Unlike many artistic pursuits, this does not manifest itself as an extension of the ego, but as a quiet, self-confident belief in our own ability.

In Zen, personal experience is everything. Zen places complete faith in inner spiritual encounters while attaching little or no importance to the authority of a didactic philosophy. In fact it is often said that in Zen there are no teachers and there is nothing to teach – because we teach ourselves and nobody can do it for us. Zen merely claims to be the finger that points the way. And when it comes to setting out on the journey of self-discovery this is certainly the case: Zen can guide and direct us, but uncovering the real truth is something we have to find out for ourselves. This is the reason why Zen teachings ultimately come from our own minds and not from others. The deep significance of this idea may be hard to grasp until it is understood that Zen only starts to make proper sense when our minds are completely free and open, uninfluenced by the opinions or prejudices of others.

Zen wants the whole mind to be totally unobstructed so it can show us the real truth unimpeded by the delusions of the ego. Once we understand this fundamental premise, we then realize why every aspect of Zen practice focuses on attaining freedom of the mind and spirit. Indeed, Zen has the potential to free us from all the useless things we acquire and those that cause misery and suffering in our lives.

No thought

no form

only emptiness . . .

the joy of silence

# meditation

In formal Zen, meditation, or *zazen* in Japanese, is the method used to attain spiritual enlightenment. And in the way that the word *Zen* ultimately derives from the Sanskrit *dhyana* (meditation), it is possible to trace the practice of meditation in Zen right back to the Buddha himself and its central role in Indian Buddhism. In fact the Buddha had adopted the method of meditation from the ancient Indian art of yoga, which was developed specifically to inspect the contents of the mind. It is therefore important to realize that meditation is not just an obscure mystical practice but a technique that has been perfected over thousands of years. In Zen today it is still practiced by both lay followers as well as those undergoing formal Zen training.

Meditation, it should be emphasized, is not easy to practice effectively. It requires correct instruction and training and, above all, it needs patience and time to learn how to control the mind and master it successfully. In perfecting the technique we are thereby able to discover what lies beyond our normal state of consciousness. And ultimately, as we progress deeper into the mind, Zen opens up the great mystery of life as it takes us to the center of our existence, the very core of our soul.

This journey into ourselves leads finally to an immense emptiness – a place without boundaries, free from all unnatural encumbrances – a place where only pure consciousness remains. For in discovering the center of the self we will discover the center of the universe . . . and in so doing attain Zen's ultimate prize: complete freedom; total enlightenment.

How do we obtain this freedom? Through the depth and insight gained from meditation we see more directly into the true nature of the self. Bit by bit we learn to let go of the built-in obstructions of conceptual thought that govern our judgments and opinions. We begin to understand that the long-established prejudices that conditioned our lives were only confining our consciousness and

imprisoning us within our minds. In time we surrender our thoughts to the exquisite experience of emptiness and in so doing set our spirit free.

The methods of spiritual training are both thorough and systematic. The Zen school has perfected a sound approach to teaching its followers how to achieve this state of enlightenment. This is where Zen's practical value should be given its due. On the one hand, Zen gives the impression of being a highly abstract approach to life, with an emphasis on inner personal experience. But when it comes down to reaching its objective, Zen uses tried-and-tested, methodical disciplines to achieve its goal.

In Zen meditation we learn to focus on a single object or thought with a fixed concentration or close focus known as *samadhi,* meaning a total oneness with the object, a single-pointedness of mind. The purpose of *samadhi* is to gather all our scattered energy and bring it into one focal point – based on the principle that once the mind is transfixed it can then be awakened.

In addition to *samadhi* there is the study of *koans*, which are practiced by the Japanese Rinzai and other sects of Zen. *Koan* study is a way of pushing us beyond our furthest limits. Its purpose is to encourage intellectual resourcefulness and to teach us to avoid using logical solutions to problems and to open up a formerly unknown region of the mind. *Koan* study ultimately enables us to surpass the concept of the self and transcend the confines of logical dualism.

When it comes to the actual practice of meditation, or *zazen*, considerable emphasis is placed on sitting in the prescribed fashion with the correct posture. We are first shown the different positions to sit in, such as the full lotus (with legs crossed and feet raised onto thighs); half lotus; cross-legged; and sitting on the heels with a cushion underneath and the knees straight ahead. It is also possible to sit upright on a high-backed chair. A straight back – one that is supported by the spinal column alone – and a low center of gravity are fundamental to all the different meditative positions. When we first learn *zazen* we begin working with our breath as a means of bringing our scattered energy into focus and calming down our thoughts. Methods include counting each breath up to ten and then repeating the process, a technique used to "distract" the mind and stop it from straying back to its normal rational thought process. As we become mindful of our breath our thoughts drop away without our realizing what is happening. Bit by bit we develop the power of concentration and learn to empty the mind of all conscious thought.

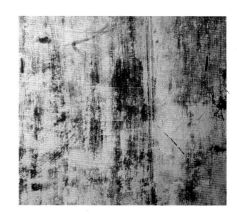

With the correct posture and proper breathing we can develop our understanding of *hara*, a Japanese word meaning "belly." This region of the body is the source of all action and initiative – it is not only the physical center but also the spiritual center of the body. Just below the navel there is a point called the *tanden*, where all the forces of the body naturally focus when allowed to function in a totally natural way. In Zen meditation, as in many martial arts, we learn to draw from this area in order to concentrate and tap its dormant energy or psycho-physical force. It is also possible that this region of the body once had special significance in Western beliefs – in anatomy it is known as the sacral region, named after the sacrum, the large wedged-shaped bone at the base of the spine that consists of five fused vertebrae. *Sacrum* is derived from the Latin word *sacer,* meaning holy, which is also the root of the word *sacred.*

In monastic life, Zen monks spend much of their day in *zazen*, often in a large room known as the *zendo* – an area set aside exclusively for this purpose. In some Zen monasteries, monks meditate facing the wall, while in others they sit facing inward. For lay Zen practitioners it is not always necessary to practice meditation in a group or class. Once the technique has been mastered it is possible to put aside a short time each day to practice alone and enjoy its benefits of relaxation and composure.

## well-being

Living Zen is about enjoying a fuller, healthier life. Zen's approach to our well-being begins with the basic wisdom that a healthy mind means a healthy body. That is why many aspects of Zen training encompass the body, mind and spirit.

The early Indian yoga influences on Zen Buddhism, combined with the more practical Chinese Taoist beliefs, have had far-reaching consequences on Zen's psycho-physical instruction. Harmony and balance in the body are central to the Chinese notions of health and well-being. And the Taoist concepts of Yin and Yang, the two opposing bodily forces animated by *ch'i* energy, the breath of life (the Japanese equivalent is *ki,* as in the martial art aikido), have shaped Zen teachings. Physical exercise too has played an essential part in the Zen curriculum. In the early Zen monasteries of China and Japan, emphasis was placed on learning martial arts such as kung fu or karate and the ancient disciplines of the Samurai warrior, such as aikido, kendo and *kyudō*. These were not specifically taught for self-defense but as a means of training the mind and body. Today, particularly in America, Zen retreats and monasteries encourage a return to these ways. Naturally, in everyday Zen it is not essential to study the martial arts. Nevertheless a regular exercise routine is encouraged.

By practicing meditation we discover many benefits beyond inducing spiritual experience – a consideration that explains its role in yoga and other relaxation exercises. When we sit quietly and concentrate on our breathing and posture, the body relaxes and the mind becomes clearer. We find our breathing becomes more regular and calm. As we grow composed, we start to take on a greater energy and vitality. It is this free-flowing energy that is one of the joys of Zen, for it allows us to appreciate fully the pleasures of everyday life. And the more we meditate, the more alive and fully awake we feel, reaching a state of total well-being.

Correct diet is another vital Zen tradition. Although the Buddha permitted the eating of meat, most Chinese Zen masters became vegetarians. This tradition arrived in

Why does the river
always know
the way?

Japan, where a style of vegetarian food called *shojin ryori* ("food for practice") was developed in Zen monasteries. Even today classic Japanese cooking is deeply rooted in these early Zen ideals and *shojin ryori* is still served in many temples. A number of Japanese staple foods such as pickles, miso and tofu originated from this Zen vegetarian diet.

The chief cook, or *tenzo*, in the former Zen monasteries of China and Japan was second only to the abbot. And in Japanese Zen retreats of today the position of cook is filled by an older, learned master, or *roshi*, who not only serves as head cook but also as a teacher and leader. The great Zen masters such as Dogen recognized that there are lessons to be found in food and the way that we prepare and eat it – many of these are contained in Dogen's practical manual *Tenzo Kyōkun (Instructions for the Zen Cook)* and its modern-day commentary *From the Zen Kitchen to Enlightenment* by Kōshō Uchiyama. And as early as the thirteenth century, Dogen set out the rules to be followed by Zen temples for the preparation and serving of vegetarian cuisine. These are still adhered to today.

Nourishment is not just putting food in our belly – it is the nourishment of our whole body and soul. "You are what you eat" is such a perceptive saying that it can be found in one way or another in almost every Eastern philosophy. How we choose, prepare and cook the food we eat affects our total well-being. That is why Zen teaches us to prepare our food with love, compassion and wisdom.

The tradition of tea drinking has long been an inseparable part of the Zen way of temple life. Tea is believed to have originated in southern Asia, brought to China by Bodhidharma in the fifth century c.e. and introduced into Japan around the same time as the arrival of Buddhism. It was originally drunk by Zen Buddhist monks both as a medicine and as a stimulant to stay awake during the long hours of praying and meditation. It was this religious background that ultimately led to the Japanese Zen tea ceremony, *cha-no-yu*. Drunk as part of a balanced diet Chinese tea or Japanese green tea (*ryokucha*) can help to promote good health and contribute to our well-being by clearing the blood and liver of harmful substances.

Sacred Fuji-san

your secrets

shrouded in the mists of time

# harmony

Most of us desire to live a natural way of life as our true selves. This is the way of Zen. At first glance, Zen may appear to be a relentless quest for spiritual enlightenment. Yet at the heart of Zen there is a clear recognition of the need for harmony and balance in life. All the methods to control the mind and the self-imposed intellectual disciplines may seem at the outset to be hard work and even quite disorientating. However, they are not there to create impediments or disturb our lives. All of these activities are fixed on one supreme goal: to take us to enlightenment and a life of great joy, harmony and understanding.

In the long run Zen's teachings are all directed at making our lives less complicated. It does this by freeing the mind of all of its clutter. To free the mind is to free the spirit. The resulting clarity of perception is just one of Zen's rewards. At every step, Zen brings us into contact with reality. There is no illusion. Only great insight.

Zen's holistic belief that you are the universe and the universe is you goes back to its Taoist origins. To understand this concept of interdependence is to unlock the door to ourselves and to realize that everything depends on everything else. The way we understand ourselves is the way we understand the universe, and these two connected worlds must constantly be kept in harmony and balance: if we are not in accord with ourselves, neither will we be in accord with the universe.

Zen understands that we are finely tuned instruments of creation who constantly need care and attention. That is why everyday Zen emphasizes a regular program of practice and why it ultimately becomes a lifelong study. Zen is forever keeping us aware and awake so that we see the world about us with an intensity and perception that heightens its beauty.

Zen's Buddhist beliefs direct us to love and cherish all living things, to respect and care for our environment and to nurture each other. In essence, living Zen is to live in harmony with the entire universe.

# zen design and architecture

Stone cold

steel gray

human warmth

# cultural and social influences

Zen reached Japan from China during the late twelfth century at a time of significant change and social upheaval. Toward the end of the Heian period (794–1185), the country's warrior class, or *bushi*, managed to wrest power away from Japan's aristocratic rulers, who, distracted by their passion for the romantic and beautiful aspects of life, had failed to address their duty of governing their subjects effectively. Now, with their harsh military samurai code and rigorous self-discipline, these new warrior rulers inaugurated a new medieval age of frugality in Japan's history.

After this shift in power from the aristocracy to military dictators, or shoguns, there followed two important periods in the development of Zen and its various manifestations. First there was the austere Kamakura era (1185–1333) under the Minamoto and Hojo families, who moved the imperial court from Kyoto to Kamakura, where much of Zen's early architecture developed. Second, after the Hojo family were eventually defeated by the Ashikaga, the seat of political power was reestablished in the Muromachi district of Kyoto, giving rise to the Muromachi or Ashikaga period (1392–1568). These two periods produced some of Japan's most renowned Zen temples, monasteries and gardens in both Kamakura and Kyoto. And despite civil war and social turmoil, these medieval times witnessed a surge of economic growth that led to an increased patronage of the arts and therefore a profound and enduring effect on Japanese culture. Although it took several centuries to become fully integrated, Zen Buddhism began to prosper in this time of austerity and military, "masculine" values.

Many of the socio-political and religious changes that took place during the Kamakura and Muromachi periods came about as a result of cultural and artistic inspiration from China, which the Japanese regarded as a source of good taste, refinement and ancient wisdom. Because Zen, or Ch'an in China, had been shaped by the naturalistic philosophy of Taoism, whose art forms aimed to capture the essence of nature, it found a welcome home among the Japanese, who already had

a comparable sense of beauty deeply rooted in their psyche. This new style of Buddhism, with its strong sense of spiritual freedom and direct simplicity, appealed to the aristocratic and warrior classes as well as to painters, poets and scholars of the time, who sought to verify their judgments and refine their sense of appreciation.

Zen's most significant impact in Japan was founded on the activities of thirteenth-century Zen masters and scholars whose cultural and political status in society allowed them to infiltrate every aspect of life. This occurred especially in the Muromachi period, when Zen became the official Buddhist religion and Zen Buddhists penetrated political councils and government circles of power. They acted as advisors to the shoguns and influenced the country's policies on education and foreign trade, as well as guiding the country's cultural development. Indeed, this cultural role meant that Zen monasteries became centers for artistic achievement and excellence – places where not only Zen monks and priests but many other artists and scholars could take refuge to pursue their work in peace, undistracted by the civil and political turmoil that was ravaging the country.

One of the great visionaries of the Kamakura period was the Zen scholar, gardener and calligrapher Muso Soseki (1275–1351), who became known by his honorary title Muso Kokushi, "Teacher of the Nation." So respected was his knowledge and wisdom that successive rulers were eager to take his advice. His influence and standing are shown by the fact that the shogun Ashikaga Takauji (1305–1358) appointed him as the first abbot of the magnificent Tenryu-ji monastery in Kyoto, which Takauji built in memory of those who perished in the war that brought the Ashikaga family to power.

In 1325 Muso Soseki persuaded the Japanese government to send an official mission to China, the first in 500 years. It was this delegation that fueled the renewed surge of Chinese artistic influence and that was to have a profound and lasting effect on the cultural heritage of Japan. The interest, however, had always been there. Because of Zen's Chinese origins, many influential Zen monks already

had a close connection with the culture of China. During the Mongol invasions, Chinese monks had sought sanctuary in Japan following the defeat of the Sung rulers of China in 1279. Later, when the Ming Dynasty was back in power and relations between the two countries were restored, Zen monks headed up the Japanese delegations that were sent to China. This meant that they played a key role in introducing mainland culture into Japan, particularly in the flourishing Ashikaga period.

Zen-inspired Chinese ideas, philosophy and art soon became the height of fashion in Japan. Many paintings, ceramics and pieces of furniture were imported from China under the direction of Zen monks, who became seen as authorities on Chinese art and culture. Zen priests not only advised the shoguns on what treasures to acquire for the Japanese court but were also arbiters of artistic taste. Many of these Zen priests were also great artists in their own right, and their influence permeated every aspect of Japanese artistic expression, from poetry, calligraphy, literature and theater to garden design, painting and architecture. Some Japanese artists of the time also mastered the brush techniques of the Chinese Sung painters and began producing ink-wash paintings of famous Chinese landscapes even though they had never visited China. These symbolic landscapes became metaphorical religious images that were used as a vehicle for Zen teachings.

By the mid-fourteenth century, Zen had become the predominant cultural and religious force in Japan and its influence is still felt today. Almost undetected, Zen has permeated every level of Japanese life, whether it is in architecture, landscape design or social behavior, and the enduring effect this has had on Japanese culture cannot be overstated. In fact, much of what is now considered to be traditional Japanese art forms or customs can be traced back to their Chinese sources during the Kamakura and Muromachi periods. Over the centuries, however, they have become so interwoven with the fabric of Japanese life that their origins have been forgotten.

# the guiding principles

To appreciate the spirit of Zen design and its influence on architecture, interiors and other art forms, it is essential to have a deeper understanding of Japanese aesthetics and a comprehension that these artistic sensibilities were shaped by Chinese culture. The overriding force on all Japanese art and design is the oriental ability to conceive life from within and not from without. This not only changes the way that things are perceived and expressed but establishes a different set of evaluative criteria based on subjective inner values and a deeper cognizance of nature. At its most fundamental level, simplicity and a love of nature lie at the core of Zen appreciation, but the Japanese aesthetic sensibility goes deeper than this.

Many of the guiding aesthetics of Zen art forms stem from the subdued taste with the concepts *wabi* and *sabi*. Originally thought to be Zen-inspired, these peculiarly Japanese, rather abstract "feelings" have penetrated every aspect of Japanese cultural life – they are often difficult to translate because of the hidden meaning and depth embodied in their subtleties and sensitivities. However, once understood they go a long way to explaining the Japanese people's intimate relationship with nature and the strong influence of Zen in shaping their affections and ideals.

*Wabi* refers to the subdued beauty inherent in simplicity and serenity and *sabi* to a refined elegance – in the way that objects become venerable and beautiful because of the patina of their age and so inspire the onlooker with a deep sense of awe. *Wabi sabi* together describes the appreciation of simple everyday items, such as tea bowls or bamboo tea whisks, which are used in a refined manner. *Wabi* might refer to the simple joys of living in a primitive straw hut – as typified by a Japanese tea house, which can create the feeling of wishing to revoke everything worldly in favor of the wonders of nature and the mystical contemplation of life. When this sense of natural simplicity is combined with a sense of antiquity or primitive rusticity it can create *sabi*.

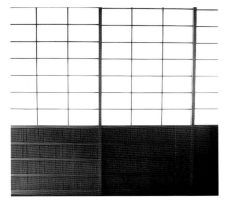

Moonlight

through a window

shadows of another world

The love of simplicity and rusticity, as expressed in *wabi sabi*, led to the appreciation of the aesthetics that surrounded the tea ceremony and consequently the influential tea cult. One of these was *sūki,* which means something that is designed in a natural way so that it shows its true nature without revealing the hard work that went into creating its beauty. Tea masters considered themselves *sūkisha* – connoisseurs who were guardians of this refined and cultivated taste and who oversaw every aspect of the tea ceremony from the choice of the tea utensils to the design of the tea garden. The principle of *shin* should also be considered in Zen design. It refers to anything that is sparse and orderly that has been created by human hands, for example a *shoji* screen or a wall plastered in special clay. *Shin* is often combined with *sō* and known as *gyō*. *Sō* describes design features that use materials in their natural state, such as a thatched bamboo roof or a tatami mat floor.

In addition to these influences, another determining principle in Zen design is the technique of *yohaku-no-bi*, meaning "the beauty of extra white." The use of this treatment can be seen in the empty spaces of Zen gardens, areas of white in Zen paintings and drawings, or the clean, uncluttered interiors of Zen rooms. This positive sense of sparseness focuses on what is left out of a design, rather than what is put in it. As such, *yohaku-no-bi* is an inherent part of the work of Japanese designers, architects and artists, modern and old, and is usually perceived as an economy of form. Its success is due to a lack of competing elements in a design or in the sparse use of brush strokes in a painting. The paradox between something that is "caught but not caught" creates a kind of dynamic tension that at first appears to be an imperfection in the design. However, when looked at more closely this method leads to a greater perception of the work's perfection. The origins of *yohaku-no-bi* can be fathomed in the very essence of Zen thought and meditation, which teach the idea of concentrating on the concepts of *ku* (emptiness) and *mu* (nothingness).

A grasp of these almost obscure ideas prepares the way for an understanding of other, even more abstract, principles that have influenced early Japanese artists.

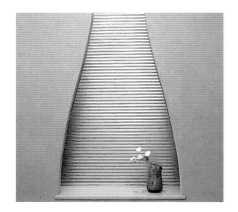

Perhaps the most elusive of these is *yugen* – a word whose Chinese precursor combines the character for "faint" or "dim" with another character for "dark" or "mysterious." Originally *yugen* referred to poetry and meant something "too deep to see," but in time it came to refer to something that is profound, subtle or abstruse, but with the suggestion of a mysterious nature. During the austere years of the Muromachi period, *yugen* was the guiding principle of aesthetic beauty, and scholars attempted through their art to reveal the true nature of reality by uncovering it from the illusory aspects of the world. As with *yohaku-no-bi*, the subtleties of *yugen* relate to things that are suggested, rather than those that are revealed or overt.

There are also other terms that convey the restraint and subtlety of Zen art. These include *shibui*, meaning reserved, sober, quiet or stringent; *koko*, meaning austere; and *kanso*, simple. Similarly, *shizen* is a concept that suggests the naturalness and closeness to nature manifested in so many Zen traditions, whether flower arranging, architecture or interior design.

Finally, there is the important concept of *fukinsei,* or asymmetry. The Japanese love of asymmetry is not easy to explain. It may stem from their origins as a race in the forests of Asia, where natural forms may have imposed a sense of organic beauty; or from the fundamental Zen belief of looking at individual things as being perfect in themselves without the need for symmetry. This is an attitude that runs largely counter to the premodern Western desire for symmetry and the orchestration of geometry to create perspective and balance. Conversely, in Zen design, asymmetry is used to create a vital force in which oppositions are set up between left and right and, often, between volume and form. In a typical Japanese design of a garden or building, the eye does not settle on any one dominant point in the design, but is constantly led back to the overall effect.

# design and architecture

Zen's distinct architectural style, while led by the aesthetics and cultural influences already mentioned, was further fueled by the early Zen monks' desire for simplicity and the need to seek tranquillity and sanctuary from the rigors of an exacting and severe existence. The disciplines of Zen itself gave rise to its own unique set of design principles that quite naturally evolved out of its frugal way of life. The understatement and clarity seen in contemporary Zen designs therefore largely originate from the need to marry function with form as the architects of the time set out to create a space for spiritual reflection and the fulfilment of inner needs.

Many of the Zen temples, monasteries and other buildings of the thirteenth century were inspired by earlier Chinese models of the Sung period (960–1279) and are constructed in the *kara-yo*, or Chinese style. Although not particularly Zen in appearance, these buildings introduced architectural notions that are still integral to Japanese architecture. For example, the meditation hall, or *zendo*, is perhaps the one room in a Zen monastery that remains the archetype of Zen's simple style. The austere nature of this large space, with its simple wooden structure, straw tatami mats and few furnishings, is virtually unchanged from the austere Kamakura era, when it originated. The natural, restrained space of the *zendo*, with its purity of form and shape, radically influenced Japanese interior design and led to the modern Zen living space as we know it today.

From the thirteenth century onward, the influence of this unpretentious Zen architecture, with its sense of spiritual freedom in harmony with nature, spread throughout Japan and impacted on the design of Japanese houses and other traditional buildings. As with architectural traditions of other countries, Japanese houses were governed by the availability of local building materials, environment and climate. Throughout Japan, abundant supplies of wood and other natural materials, such as clay, reeds and paper – which all have a capacity for low heat absorption – were used to counteract the warm humidity and relatively high frequency of earthquakes.

However, the type of building that embodies most of these fundamental Zen inspirations is not so much religious as secular – namely, the teahouse, or *chashitsu*. This modest, simple structure originates from the latter half of the sixteenth century and is built with natural materials in the primitive style of a peasant's hut. The interior is almost completely bare. The floor is covered with tatami mats; the walls are made of natural wood and a mud-clay mix finished to look like plaster. The ceiling is often constructed from bamboo or strips of wood or bark. As windows, *shoji* screens of rice paper create a soft diffuse light that adds to the feeling of tranquillity. The low entrance, or *nijiriguchi*, is designed to make those who are invited inside feel humble: guests literally have to crawl into the tea room – an action that signifies that all social distinctions and worldly pride are to be left behind on entering this "world of tea."

Architectural conventions such as these have become so much part of Japanese design that their Zen origins are often forgotten. When Japanese people compare the clean, simple lines of their homes with the clutter often found in Western interiors, they do not consciously connect their tradition of simplicity specifically with Zen. Rather, they think of a more general aesthetic heritage – in a way that indicates how deeply the Japanese psyche has been imbued with the spirit of Zen.

From the 1930s onward, principles of Zen design began to reach the West, influencing the German Bauhaus movement and pioneering architects such as the German-born Ludwig Mies van der Rohe and Walter Gropius. Zen's influence can also be seen in the work of the American Frank Lloyd Wright, the Frenchman Le Corbusier, and the Finnish designer Alvar Aalto. Furthermore, Zen has also inspired a number of leading contemporary architects and designers, such as Charles and Ray Eames, Verner Panton, Jean Nouvel, John Pawson and Richard Rogers. By conveying a spirit of purity of form in their work, contemporary Japanese architects also continue to reflect the centuries-old influence of Zen. Modern-day architects such as the brilliant Tadao Ando and other designers like Fumihiko Maki, Toyo Ito and Itsuko Hasegawa continue to use the principles and dynamics of Zen in their architecture.

# living spaces

The aim of the Zen living space is to embody Zen's free spirit and the lifestyle it evokes. At the core of Zen design is a great sense of freedom tempered by the aesthetic restraints of simplicity and understatement. This results in a great clarity of expression and boldness of style.

One of the most distinctive aspects of Zen design is its pared-down simplicity. The Zen living space is a deliberate attempt to rid our lives of clutter and unnecessary distractions or belongings. This has the effect of bringing into sharper focus the beauty and quality of the carefully selected furnishings and materials that are the central components of the design. Zen could have easily coined the adage "less is more," but it recognizes that what is "less" must be more beautiful – and more perfect. Zen's understated approach, allied with its principle of *yohaku-no-bi*, brings into even sharper focus the quality of the design and the architectural aspects of the space: with a clean, uncluttered canvas that serves to highlight the intense beauty of all that remains, Zen enables the eye to be drawn to detail that might otherwise have been overlooked.

Zen design may sometimes be perceived as a celebration of the austere and sober. But this is not the case. Its aim is to avoid excesses of eclecticism while providing the right stimulation for free artistic thought and expression. Far from being sterile, Zen interiors are places of inspiration, catalysts for new ideas – places where creativity can flow and originality come to the fore.

Although distinguished by its simplicity, the Zen interior is not necessarily easy to design. Harmony and balance are the overriding considerations – in accordance with the holistic principles on which the Zen home is based. Zen design, as with any other successful design, stresses the importance of the right dimensions and balance between form and function. However, few designers can achieve this vision unless they have fully understood Zen's ability to reach down to the inner essence and see things as they really are with an eye for the smallest detail.

Zen interiors are organic, functional, free-flowing spaces that should liberate the thoughts of their occupants. Although straight lines and geometric patterns are primary elements, neither the mind nor the eye should be boxed in by symmetrical shapes or bored by repetitious elements. The purity and uncomplicated appeal of Zen design can be lost if too many shapes or angles are added.

The Zen interior has been closely linked to minimalism. In many areas there are parallels – but Zen design is not reliant on stark sensationalism to make a statement or on simply being ultra-modern. When it comes to comfort, modern Zen design does not insist on its early monastic origins. Living spaces are after all for living in and not for religious enlightenment. This means that unlike many bare minimalist interiors, the Zen living space is comfortable as well as being functional. Its fresh, noncontrived approach harmonizes aesthetics with practicality – making it a place for living in, not a designer showcase. And although Zen interiors are associated with modernism, antiques have a place in their repertoire, as does a fusion of contemporary and classic styles – often a mixture of Eastern and Western tastes in which the best of both aesthetic worlds contributes to the overall effect.

The universal ingredient of the well-designed Zen interior is light. Although this can be said to apply to all living spaces, since natural light enhances any setting, in the uncluttered interiors of Zen homes the quality of ambient light becomes even more critical – to emphasize form, shape and space. Light also creates a sense of harmony and positive energy: in modern Zen interiors dark, dingy spaces are avoided at all costs since the Zen experience – as with all spiritual experiences – has a strong dependence on the purity of light.

The light in Zen-designed rooms of old was usually diffused by the use of paper screens known as *shoji*. This produced a soothing, spiritual quality and created a tranquil environment for meditation or quiet contemplation. In modern Zen interiors, harsh sunlight is often softened or diffused through opaque, smoked or sand-blasted glass windows or, alternatively, filtered through translucent screens or slatted blinds. Above all, the source of light has a crucial influence in creating a

tranquil atmosphere and making us feel totally at ease with our surroundings. With its purity and vitality, it can even make rooms feel like sacred spaces or spiritual refuges.

The modern Zen home is not always austere in its choice of colors. Its purpose is to select a palette that evokes serenity and harmony while avoiding a clash of conflicting shades. Since its conception, Zen design has drawn on nature for inspiration, and this guiding aesthetic is still central today. In keeping with contemporary trends, base colors tend to be subtle shades of white erring toward cream, beige, straw, ochre and sand colors, along with other warm natural tones. These are often combined with soft pastels, such as pale blues or washes of green – which are also found in nature's more subdued palette. Where contrast is required, richer, earthier colors are applied. In turn, Zen often uses wood, with all its infinite shades, in its structures, fittings and furnishings. Black is also carefully employed to create strong contrasts or to highlight the details within a room.

Some modern Zen-influenced designers have tried to achieve a greater sense of balance by introducing all the five different natural elements into their work. Water, earth, wood and metal – and even fire, when used mindfully – all add an extra dynamic to the Zen interior and utilize the natural patterns and energies that are at work around us. Importantly, they embody the Zen emphasis on closeness to nature and attest to the Japanese love of *yugen*, or hidden symbolism.

The Japanese tradition of using natural materials remains central to the Zen living space. This not only provides for a more eco-sensitive environment but creates an intense focus on the quality and beauty of the materials used. Living in a home made from natural materials such as wood, textiles and stone are Zen traditions that continue to provide pleasure and stimulate the senses. The Zen interior must convey a sense of *wabi* and *sabi* through the patina of age and the innate harmony derived from the interaction of different textures and natural finishes.

The Zen living space is in tune with the current fashion for "eco-chic." The two, in fact, are one and the same. Zen's deep respect for all living things and its concern for the environment naturally lead to an eco-friendly house and lifestyle. And although Zen designers revere natural materials, they consider carefully every aspect of the interior, avoiding wood from endangered trees and materials or adornments that are made from animals. They try to employ local resources to avoid transportation and they endeavor to recycle materials when they can and use water and fossil fuels sparingly.

In the spirit of Zen the beauty of the actual nature of the materials is highly valued, such as the texture or pattern of a fabric, a delicate color or hue in a wood floor or the patina of a piece of furniture. This is a tradition that originates from the early Zen temples where the natural grain or pattern of wood was treasured and where great care was taken in the workmanship of all the furnishings to highlight these qualities. Even the most basic of natural materials were molded and beautified for use in design, including bamboo, reeds, clay mud, rice paper and Japanese cedar wood.

In a pared-down environment texture plays a central role. A space that contains only the bare essentials seems to accentuate the sensuality of its surfaces and finishes. In the simple surroundings of a Zen interior the texture of a fabric or other soft furnishing becomes more evident. Similarly the finish of hard surfaces such as a stone floor is much more pronounced. This means that great care should be taken in selecting materials for Zen living spaces so that they not only match in color but create a pleasing contrast in finish and feel. As with everything in Zen there are no hard and fast rules. However, texture and touch are inseparable experiences in a natural Zen interior, where opposing sensations such as hot and cold and rough and smooth are often exploited to great effect. These rooms should be explored with all the senses.

The early Japanese domestic interiors were completely shaped by religious architecture as the builders of the day strove to capture the spirit of Zen, with its

Taoist-derived feeling for nature. This in turn gave birth to the Zen-inspired Japanese house known as *shoin-zukuri*, which evolved in the Muromachi period. It replaced the old-style *shinden-zukuri* and gave rise to a new style of residence that incorporated the bold characteristics found in the austere culture of the Zen monks and the *bushi*, the new warrior class. Because of the influence of Zen on daily life, architects equipped the *shoin-zukuri* with many of the features found in a *hojo*, the residence of a Zen abbot. For example, the *shoin* (from which the name of this type of architecture is derived) was a window-style desk that often formed part of a small study. There was also the *toko* or *tokonoma* – an alcove with a raised platform that is today used for displaying works of art or flower arrangements and, as it was used in the past, for exhibiting Buddhist scrolls written in fine calligraphy. In addition, there was the *tana* – a shelf built into the wall to house scrolls and sacred texts; when translated into the home, it became used for storage.

Other borrowed monastic features include *shoji* screens and tatami mats as well as the entrance hall, or *genkan*, a classic feature of the Japanese house. However, it was the sheer simplicity and clean, unadorned design of monasteries that had the most impact on these house designers and symbolized for them the true tradition of Zen. Finally, it should be stressed that in the same way that Zen, as a belief system, had no hard and fast rules, the Zen designers of the period were also free to experiment: the only constraints were Zen's insistence on a calm, serene environment, where nature dictated the theme and eclectic clutter was avoided. Many of these features are still present in the modern Japanese-style house – often reinterpreted or modernized, but all springing from the same religious origins.

Zen temple

in my soul

sacred source of peace

# spiritual sanctuary

The religious origins of Zen architecture and design have influenced a whole new style of decor that has a profound spiritual presence. The sense of calm and harmony found in Zen's simple, natural style more often than not transmits the same feel to its occupants. The contemporary Zen interior has evolved organically to be more than just a living space: through the ritual of meditation and our own personal forms of liturgy it has become a modern-day refuge where we can seek peace in spiritual reflection and achieve fulfilment of our inner needs.

The very early Zen interior designers had motives similar to those we have today – the Japanese monks and priests who created the Zen interior style were driven by the same desire to escape the pressures and distractions of a demanding world. Their prime purpose was to create an oasis of calm so that they could single-mindedly pursue their goal of enlightenment. In keeping with Zen tradition they sought stimulation from the simple joys of nature and absorption in performing everyday tasks.

Unlike the outlook of architects in other religions, there was no metaphysical or mystical aspect in these Zen designers' motives. The first Zen interiors were not conceived as houses of worship designed for ancient ceremony or religious rites. They were not the same as the "Buddha rooms" of other sects, filled with ritual icons or sacred idols; nor were they hallowed temples for revering a higher power or deity. Instead they were unadorned, self-effacing spaces designed purely with one aim in mind – to aid enlightenment. Simplicity and serenity were therefore the determining factors. Today, these carefully considered spaces in the temples of Japan remain havens of calm and reassurance where the entire mind, body and spirit can feel a sense of integration with the essential nature of Zen.

Through Zen, our homes can become our own sacred space. The plainness and beauty found in Zen expression make our living space a sanctuary for the soul, where we can escape the discord and stress of modern life. Zen provides a place

where we can seek new meaning for our lives and restore the balance – a place for quiet contemplation where we can nurture stillness and search for inner truth.

Many people who practise Zen at home create their own physical space for meditation or spiritual repose. This does not have to be a special room but simply a corner of a room – where there is a sense of calm and seclusion – set aside for this purpose. Some people often choose to sit in contemplation near a window overlooking a garden or a view of nature – whereas others prefer fewer distractions. Essentially it is important to keep the space uncomplicated – as simple as possible. This should be an area of the home where you can focus on your Zen practice and allow yourself to be completely centered.

Some create home altars on which they place flowers, incense and candles. Other objects might include a bowl of water, so that the four elements of earth, fire, air and water are present. A statue of Buddha can also be used as a central image, and other cherished icons, such as photographs of loved ones or special mementoes, can also be placed there. However, as with everything else in Zen, the basic rule is to keep it simple.

Inner exploration is not all that the Zen sacred space offers. Inspiration and stimulation are its other aims. The immediacy and vitality in Zen serve to nourish the soul and lift the spirit. Its boldness of style induces clarity of thought and feeds the creative process. Natural materials enhanced by nature's beauty arouse the senses and create the balance and harmony that come from positive, free-flowing energy. The feel of different textures becomes a more sensuous experience: the Zen interior is mindful of the need to connect us with our more primitive instincts.

# objects and adornments

Zen's spirit of freedom encourages the belief that fewer possessions mean fewer problems. Zen's pared-down style has evolved from the desire of its faithful to rid themselves of all unnecessary material trappings. However, in common with Zen scholars and monks of old, many modern Zen devotees value beautiful objects or works of art and try to display them in such a way that their innermost beauty can be fully appreciated.

Zen awareness helps us to see beyond the form of an object to discover its hidden value. For Zen teaches that the key to understanding beauty in a work of art is to break through to its spirit by a process of total self-immersion. The clean, meticulous décor of Zen sharpens our powers of observation and heightens the beauty of even the most common everyday objects. Colors, shapes, textures and craftsmanship all take on a new vitality and we begin to see hidden beauty in things we might have taken for granted in a more cluttered, confused environment.

Zen designers find objects or ornaments made from natural materials the most appealing. For nature is Zen's favorite subject and has been – as it still is – the inspiration of all its art forms and expressions. Simple, natural objects, such as stones or driftwood from a beach, or dried seed pods, become a source of wonder – as do hand-finished ceramics created from natural clays and glazes, or wooden objects that emphasize the grain and texture of the wood. Traditional Japanese flower arranging, known as *ikebana*, with its emphasis on simple, natural arrangements can be adapted to modern styles so that flowers are shown to their full beauty.

Objects from the East provide a strong Zen flavor but are not essential for styling a modern Zen living space. Zen's fusion of styles means that East and West find equal favor; overall there should be just a few well-chosen pieces that add harmony and balance to the home.

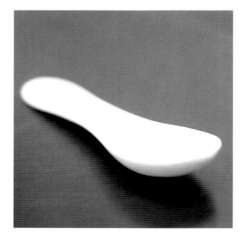

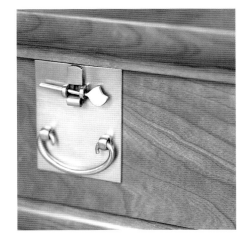

# the zen garden

Stone, sand and rock
reveal the mysteries
of time

# a brief history

Nowhere do we see more clearly the deep, pervasive influence Zen Buddhism had on Japanese culture than in the Zen garden. To understand the spiritual essence of this unique style of landscaping it helps to know the geographical conditions in which Zen gardens originated, as well as the complex forces of nature and society that shaped their form.

Japan's archipelago consists of a long, narrow string of islands positioned on the eastern edge of the tectonic plates that form the Asian continent. More than 75 percent of Japan's landmass is mountainous, while the rest of the country is mainly composed of steep, sloping valleys and narrow, coastal plains. The warm maritime climate and frequent rainfall of these islands create moist, humid conditions that support a rich diversity of flora. This close climate combined with the constrictions caused by Japan's lack of habitable land has had a marked impact on garden design as well as on the country's society and culture. Agriculture, too, has played its part: the introduction in the first century C.E. of wet rice farming – which requires terracing and agrarian ingenuity – dramatically changed the landscape and marked the first attempts to control nature.

Apart from the role of nature, the earliest influences on the Japanese garden are thought to derive from Chinese gardens first created some five thousand years ago. The ancient tradition of Taoist landscapes, imbued with symbolism, was eventually introduced into Japan via Korea in the seventh century C.E., establishing the core design principles of the early Zen gardens. Zen Buddhism, however, did not arrive in Japan until the late twelfth century, and it was probably not until about 1250, during the Kamakura era (1185–1333), that the Zen-influenced garden started to become apparent. Even then, a strong Chinese influence remained in the way these new temple courtyard gardens were conceived. For, in the same way that the Japanese warrior rulers of the time looked to their mainland counterparts as a source of inspiration and cultural stimulation, so also were many artistic activities and artifacts imported from China and copied and refined.

The sociopolitical forces in the Kamakura period also helped to shape the prevailing aesthetic of the time and further the appeal of Zen. The control of the country by the *bushi* – the harsh, disciplined warrior class – brought about a new age of severity and masculine values that was expressed in the country's architecture, landscaping and artistic endeavors. In Zen, Japan's intellectual elite found a higher affirmation of life and a way of surpassing the trivialities of the world and finding hidden spiritual truths. At the outset, Zen "landscapes," mainly situated in the grounds of Zen temples, may have been regarded not so much as gardens but as understated symbolic spaces created for the purpose of deepening Zen beliefs. They were probably first and foremost religious works of art, designed to depict images with a hidden spiritual message.

By the time the prosperous Muromachi period arrived in 1392, this allegorical form of garden design was being expressed with even greater purpose and what we now consider to be the true Zen garden began to materialize. As designers struggled to create a balance between the life-giving forces that controlled the natural world and the harmony and order implicit in Zen, they developed an even more abstract style of gardening. The key elements that they used were simplicity and suggestiveness; and these two qualities led them to create gardens with a sort of stylized naturalism designed to forge a deeper affinity between man and nature and to instill an appreciation of everyday things.

Above all, these garden designers wanted to provide a physical setting for quiet contemplation and meditation. The garden was a place where priests, scholars, noblemen or warriors could find respite from the rigors of everyday life. Here, in a haven of calm, designed to express a deeper understanding of Zen principles, they could heighten their awareness of beauty and commune with the natural world while pursuing their goal of Zen enlightenment.

Because the early Zen gardens were markedly understated, they did not resemble the more stylized Japanese gardens better known today. Ornamental icons such as stone lanterns, water basins or stepping stones – typically associated with classical Japanese garden design – were later additions from the tea gardens of Azuchi-Momoyama times (1568–1600) and the following Edo period. By contrast, the first Japanese Zen garden designers – mainly monks and Zen scholars – were more austere in their taste. Their constant search for inner truth in the external world made them disdainful of superficial or overdecorated art forms. They did, of course, prize beauty and artistry; but religious and spiritual expression, with its simplicity and spareness, was the driving force behind the creation of these unique landscapes.

Many early Buddhist temple gardens were allegorical – they were designed to reflect the religious teachings of Zen and were probably used to convey Buddhist precepts; they also impersonated the mythical landscapes of ancient China. Features with a spiritual meaning included dry-stone waterfalls, such as the famous "dragon's gate" in the temple garden Tenryu-ji, which represented the story of the struggle of life with the Chinese parable of a giant carp that was transformed into a dragon when it made it to the top of a waterfall. Other more popular themes were the symbolic images of mountains and deep hidden valleys in faraway lands that signified the origin of life and the source of all truth.

Bridges, known as *bashi* in Japanese, were also more than functional elements in the Zen garden. They were allegorical because they were seen to link two worlds – often that of man and the gods or heaven and earth. This symbolism was used in the dry contemplation gardens of Zen temple courtyards where rough stone bridges were sometimes built over sand raked to look like the flowing water of a river. Stone bridges, like those in the gardens of Daisen-in and Zuihō-in at Daitoku-ji temple, implied the passing of man from the physical world into a higher spiritual state of consciousness.

# sand, stone and water

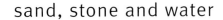

Although Zen gardens came in many forms, including landscaped parks and stroll gardens, those most associated with Zen are the dry sand-and-stone spaces originally found in medieval temple courtyards. Influenced by the period's preference for austerity and simplicity, this symbolic style of gardening is known as *kare-san-sui* (dry-mountain-water). The term refers to the way mountains are represented in the garden by carefully selected rocks; and water by sand that has been raked to give it the pattern of waves or flowing water.

In fact, this style of landscaping existed before the Middle Ages and the arrival of Zen in Japan. Areas of sand and stone had been used to create effects in the larger gardens of the Heian period (794–1185) – gardens where people could walk around and commune with nature. Moreover, since time immemorial, rocks had been used in Japanese garden design because they were thought to contain the spirits of gods or to have special powers. However, with the advent of Zen temple architecture in the Muromachi period (1392–1568), these garden elements found a new context and purpose since the new temple gardens were not so much designed for setting foot in as for spiritual exploration. These gardens were not, however, used primarily for meditation – but rather for contemplation and spiritual encouragement. Their physical setting, in courtyards or outdoor enclosures, combined with their proximity to the *zendo,* or meditation hall, made them suitable for contemplation, as their name *kansho-teien* (contemplation gardens) implies. In short, these temple gardens differed entirely from gardens designed purely for physical enjoyment or for beauty: they were, instead, designed exclusively as profound expressions of Zen philosophy and as a means to self-examination and the path to enlightenment.

The regular maintenance and raking of these temple gardens occupied an important role in temple life. Despite the artistry and skill involved, however, this duty was regarded with other daily tasks simply as a means to an end. The requisite concentration and attention to detail had an essentially meditative value and represented yet another step down the road to enlightenment.

Perhaps the best known example of a Zen contemplation garden is the sand-and-stone garden of Ryoan-ji in Kyoto. Created in about 1499, it is often referred to as a sermon in stone because it so visibly embodies many tenets of Zen belief. The beauty of this garden is subtle but awesome. Its inherent *yugen* – depth of mystery and tranquillity – is complemented by the balance achieved through the relationship of the size, position and grouping of its rocks. The combined effect is a feeling of dynamic movement: the garden is like a river flowing with a rhythm and purpose surpassed only by its harmony of color and texture, and truly epitomizes the way Zen garden design presents its esoteric spiritual message in sand and rock. Ryoan-ji is the supreme example of how Zen can provide parables not in words but through symbolism and aesthetic expression.

The empty space evident at Ryoan-ji and other Zen gardens – which is conveyed by the term *mu* (nothingness) – has the effect of heightening our appreciation of the composition. *Mu* is a central precept of Zen design and leads to the concept of *ma* – a more subtle term that refers to the space or focal point that is framed by the balancing elements. This accent on the spatial relationship is like a punctuation device creating moments of visual silence as a reprieve for the eye and the mind in a setting conceived for contemplation. It expresses perfectly the important concept of *yohaku-no-bi*, with its implication of beauty found in paucity, which is widely used in Zen art forms.

Another determining factor in the design of *kare-san-sui* gardens was the imported Chinese art of miniature "tray" landscapes, known as *kazan* or *kazansui*. These artificial landscapes, known in the West as bonsai (tray planting), were created from sand and little rocks and the occasional dwarfed plant placed inside small, flat containers often made of stone or bronze. Making these miniature landscapes became a popular Japanese pastime during the Muromachi period and their resemblance to *kare-san-sui* gardens suggests they were a principal inspiration for this new, definitive style of gardening.

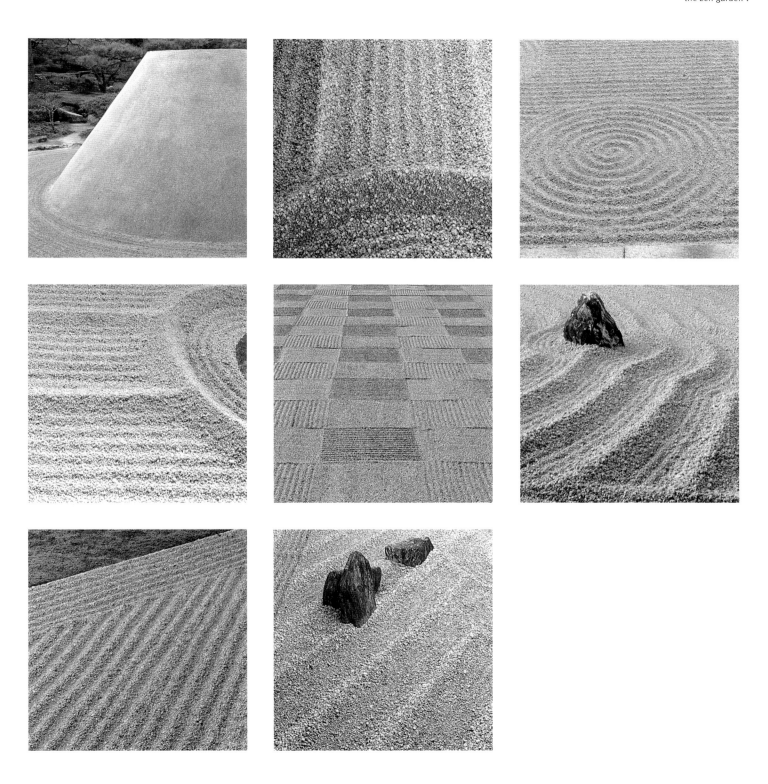

# the great within the small

Although this new style of landscaping arose from the austere culture of the Kamakura period (1185–1333), it was not until the Muromachi period (1392–1568), that a distinct natural theme started to occur in garden design along with the spiritual tenets of Zen. Inspired by Chinese art, it became increasingly fashionable to have a garden that echoed the naturalism and spiritual content of ink-wash (*sumi-e*) Taoist landscape paintings of the earlier Sung dynasty. Many Zen monks who traveled between China and Japan brought back these much admired artworks, which were then copied and studied by Japanese students.

In these symbolic landscapes, painters set out to express man's innate harmony with nature and his relationship with the cosmos. They skillfully conveyed through their deft brushwork the sense that everything flowed according to a natural order based on principles of Yin and Yang. Their paintings – which often show a solitary hut or refuge of a reclusive scholar set in a vast landscape of mountains and rivers – appealed to the taste at the time for things that revealed inner truth.

The stylized representation of mountains and rivers by rocks and raked sand became the blueprint for the Muromachi Zen garden. Using ingenuity and imagination, Zen designers re-created the concept of these idealized paintings as gardens that became microcosms of a vast landscape. On a small scale the elements of the natural world were cleverly used to give the illusion of a greater outdoor space. A sense of dimension and depth was achieved through the skillful layering of stones, which were also used as the equivalents of dynamic brush strokes and application of line in paintings. The gardens' empty spaces mimicked the Chinese artists' use of unpainted areas in their compositions, while the employment of monochromatic materials such as sand, rocks and stones mirrored the tonal values of the original Sung ink-wash paintings. This technique of compressing a vast landscape into a small space became known as the great within the small and from the Muromachi period onward it influenced many other forms of Japanese garden design.

# the tea garden

During the Middle Ages, the spiritual force of Zen Buddhism and the cultural influences of mainland China became established in Japan. One of the most significant new Zen-influenced pastimes was the practice of drinking tea, which gave rise to *chadō* or *sadō* – "the way of tea." This in turn led to the Japanese tea ceremony, *cha-no-yu*, and the ascetic art form of the tea garden.

It is said in Japan, "To study the way of tea is to study Zen." This implies that everything concerning *chadō* is a way of training both body and mind in the rigorous spiritual disciplines of formal Zen practice. But the saying also alludes to the role that Zen played in furthering the culture of tea drinking, which was closely connected with Zen temple life.

It was in fact through Zen Buddhism that tea drinking in China and Japan first developed. The Indian Buddhist missionary Bodhidharma is reputed to have introduced tea into China. From there, because of its value both as a medicine and a stimulant for religious concentration, it found its way to Japan through Buddhist monks involved in the trade between the two countries. But although tea was drunk in Japan as early as the sixth century, it did not become firmly established until the Kamakura period (1185–1333). This came about after the first Zen priest, Eisai, brought tea plants back to Japan. For he realized while studying Zen in China that tea was an indispensable part of Zen tradition and temple life.

By the end of the Muromachi period (1392–1568) and the beginning of the Momoyama period (1568–1600), the ritual of tea drinking, under the guidance of tea masters such as Sen-no-Rikyu and his grandson Sen-no-Sotan, had changed dramatically. Under the restraint of Zen, the tea ceremony changed from a lavish, festive event, often celebrated in palaces or affluent surroundings, to the ascetic art form of *wabi-cha*. This was held in the simple, rustic surroundings of a small teahouse – usually a thatched hut known as a *soan*. Expensive tea utensils once imported from China were replaced by more plain, rustic earthenware ceramics

from Korea. And emphasis was now placed on a heightened awareness of nature and the appreciation of beauty and rusticity in its simplest expression.

The tea garden, or *cha-niwa,* was first designed as a pathway or approach to the teahouse and not as place to drink tea. From this original function it acquired its name *roji,* which originally meant "alleyway" and then came to mean "dewy ground," with the association of dampness and shade, moss and stones. Through the introduction of plants and ornaments, the *roji* – this teahouse pathway – ultimately developed into a highly stylized garden that became an inseparable part of *chadō.* The garden's physical setting became a prelude to the more intense focus of the teahouse, with its underlying Zen disciplines; and it provided an escape from the distractions of everyday life and a transition from them to the spiritual demands and rituals of the tea ceremony. Through suggestion and design, the *roji* came to symbolize a compressed spiritual journey that transported the visitor to a place expressive of timeless serenity, where people could leave worldly cares behind and seek the spiritual solitude of a hermit's hut.

Because the tea garden was designed to embody the progress from a busy town street to a reclusive rustic setting, it was often divided into two sections to convey this transition. Physical and symbolic barriers were represented by gates and thresholds. These included the *soto-mon,* which usually formed the entrance from the street into the outer *roji*; and the *chu-mon,* a light gate that comprised the entrance to the inner *roji.* The outer *roji* represented the world nearest to civilization, whereas the inner *roji* was the part farthest away, where nature was less controlled.

Apart from representing a spiritual passage, the traditional tea garden contained a number of elements, such as stepping stones, a stone lantern and a stone water basin, that have become typical features of most modern Japanese gardens. Many of these ornaments were introduced by tea masters for practical purposes during the more elaborate times of the sixteenth century. Over the course of time, they gained a deep symbolic significance.

The artistic use of stepping stones, or *tobi-ishi*, originally served to protect people's feet and the plants as well as provide a naturalistic path through the garden. Lanterns became a necessity in the Momoyama period (1568–1600), when the tea ceremony was often held at night. Popular votive offerings at temples and shrines from early Buddhist days, stone lanterns, or *ishidōrō*, were gradually introduced into tea gardens both for their aesthetic appeal and their usefulness. In many cases, lanterns were taken from disused places of worship and placed in gardens; sometimes, however, the more resourceful tea masters designed and carved their own stone lanterns, which today have become highly prized objects.

Mossy path

green, green, green,

welcome rain

Other elements of the tea garden included a well, known as an *ido*, to draw water for tea making and a *chiri-ana*, a small pit lined with roof tiles where the dirt and dead leaves of the tea garden were swept during the ritual clearing of the area prior to a tea ceremony.

The tea masters' insistence on cleanliness resulted in the inclusion of the stone basin or *chozubachi* (hand-washing bowl). This basin, together with a number of other stones, each with a specific function, formed the *tsukubai* – a receptacle for washing the hands and mouth before entering a teahouse. This ritual act came to represent the symbolic cleansing of the mind and was based on the belief that true and natural beauty would not be revealed if there was the taint of impurity.

The planting of the tea garden was intended to be as close to nature as possible and to evoke the atmosphere of mountains. The bare ground was usually covered with moss, which occurred naturally in many parts of Japan and was possibly not always intended by the creator of the garden. Usually designers chose evergreen shrubs and trees that were kept tightly under control and had a simple appearance. Deciduous or flowering shrubs and trees with dramatic color were shunned while plants that were part of the natural ecology, such as ferns and grasses, were encouraged.

# the moss gardens of kyoto

The exquisite and delicate moss gardens in the Zen temple gardens of Kyoto were probably created by accident. It is likely that these areas were once bare ground or unused spaces in the temple courtyards. For in the humid, clammy conditions of Kyoto, where moss spores are everywhere in the air and are quick to get established, any patch of ground left unattended for short periods of time will soon be covered with moss.

Kyoto's striking moss gardens are known to have been added to the Zen temple precincts later than the austere, classical *kare-san-sui* gardens. Few plants were used in the manicured Zen gardens of medieval times; but moss by its very nature was able to establish itself quite naturally. Over the years, however, the Zen monks who attended to these spaces realized the inherent beauty of moss and began to create gardens that almost entirely focused on this natural groundcover as the central feature. Verdant and lush all year round, moss was used as an element of natural design, particularly in combination with rocks, stepping stones or paths.

In the Zen garden, moss came to symbolize the abundance of life itself and the richness and fullness of the Buddhist religion. Moss was frequently used as an integral part of the *kare-san-sui* garden, often to represent forests of tall trees around the base of mountains or islands embodied by carefully selected rocks. Ultimately, whole areas of the temple courtyards were set aside solely for the cultivation of moss gardens. Today these areas of moss are highly prized and great care is taken to ensure their continuation.

One of the most beautiful and well-documented Zen moss gardens is the checkerboard or *ichimatsu* pattern garden at the famous Zen temple of Tofuku-ji. Here the texture of the moss planted between square slabs of old stone is complemented by clipped azalea bushes, which are designed to break up the geometry of the regimented squares. Perhaps the most famous Buddhist moss garden – although it is not strictly a Zen garden – can be found at Saiho-ji in Kyoto. Often called the Moss Temple or Koke-dera, this is a park-style "stroll garden" and differs from the inner courtyard moss gardens of many other Zen temples.

Big rocks

on the riverbed

water soothes the soul

# zen gardens for today

The fundamental principles used 800 years ago in creating Zen gardens are still valid today. *Kare-san-sui* gardens, using rocks and raked sand, and other similar designs that derive from the Japanese tea garden, continue to be created in many different countries, remaining remarkably faithful to their Japanese models. For although in many cases the religious significance and allegorical nature of the garden has been forgotten, the appearance has altered little from Muromachi times.

The continuing appeal of this type of Zen garden is largely due to the exceptional beauty found in Zen simplicity. Since its conception, Zen's clean, bold approach has never really gone out of fashion – perhaps because it has the virtue of complementing any style of architecture that seeks to create a similar effect of simplicity. As a result, principles of the traditional Zen garden have impacted on many schools of modern Western garden design – not least the work of late nineteenth-century landscape architects, who, driven by the need to marry function and form, borrowed ideas from Zen's direct approach.

In the same way that it had a profound influence on modern architecture, Zen also inspired the layout and design of the immediate surroundings of a building. Pioneering modernist architects, such as Mies van der Rohe and Walter Gropius, as well as Le Corbusier and Berthold Lubetkin, often designed the landscapes connected with their buildings. A good example of this unity of conception is Le Corbusier's roof terrace on top of the Villa Savoye outside Paris – an inspired piece of work that echoes the geometry and illusion of space and form found in classical Zen gardens.

Many of the contemporary landscapes that accompanied the new twentieth-century modernist architecture dispensed with the formality, structure and symmetry then prevalent in traditional European landscaping. Partly through the influence of Zen, the entire fabric of the garden changed. Conventional, hard landscaping materials such as brick and stone were dispensed with in favor of synthetic processed

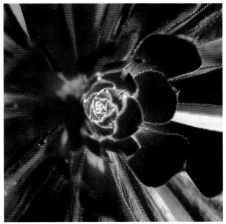

Horses' hooves –

eyes white in the dark

sparks on the cobbles

materials. Also, planting design became streamlined and less fussy. In an almost minimalist style of landscaping, plants now had to provide not only color but also architectural shape and form. And the emphasis shifted from growing mixtures of different plants to planting large areas with just one species.

Until recently in Europe, modernist landscapes were designed almost exclusively for public or institutional buildings – and perhaps a few private houses belonging to the wealthy. Moreover, because many garden designers had been given a conventional horticultural training and had been raised on traditional formal ideas of design, the creation of innovative Zen-inspired gardens was restricted. However, at the start of the new millennium, there is fresh interest in modern-style gardens in parallel with a trend toward eco-chic interiors that use natural, environmentally friendly materials. Many house owners, for example, are now restructuring their gardens to complement the interiors of their houses, sometimes by extending their living space outward with "outdoor rooms."

It is clear, however, that modern Zen-inspired gardens – both in the West and in Japan – have to make concessions. For example, the more esoteric aesthetics that guided the original Zen gardens will probably have little bearing on today's design approach; and climate and availability of building materials will impose their own conditions. Even so, Zen gardens are adapting to meet the needs of modern society. Although they are no longer seen as religious expressions, they nevertheless remain relevant as places for contemplation, escape and refuge – safety valves in today's high-pressure world. Moreover, in the future, Zen gardens can take on another, even more vital role in improving the environment in our increasingly urbanized way of life. Evolving from the compressed spaces of temple courtyards and town-house tea gardens, they contain invaluable lessons on how to incorporate successfully the elements of the natural world into confined urban environments.

# learning from the lotus

For centuries, the lotus flower has been celebrated in the literature, poetry and decorative arts of many different Asian cultures. And even before the birth of Buddhism, the incomparable beauty of the flower had a marked influence on Eastern philosophy and religion. The Chinese called it the *ho* (harmony) flower, and it was used as an emblem by Ho Hsien-ku, one of the Eight Immortals of Taoist mythology. And ever since the day the Buddha held up a lotus flower while teaching his disciples on Vulture Peak, its symbolism and imagery have been deeply rooted in Buddhist beliefs. Whether in sacred sutras or chanted mantras, the heavenly lotus flower has become a metaphor for the mystery of life.

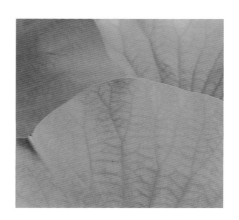

Raindrops –
like silver pearls of wisdom
adorn the lotus leaf

Today in Japan and other parts of the East, the Asian lotus (*Nelumbo nucifera*) continues to be cultivated in Zen Buddhist monasteries and temple gardens as a sacred flower and a living symbol of peace and perfection. And in one of the more widely taught Zen *koans*, or short instructional stories, it is shown how the lotus can help us see the true nature of reality:

> A monk once asked the great Zen master Chimon, "What will the
> lotus flower be when it has not yet come out of the water?"
> "The lotus flower," said Chimon.
> "What will it be when it is out of the water?" the monk then asked.
> "The lotus leaves," Chimon replied.

This response from a wise old Zen master teaches us to transcend our normal powers of perception and understand the transient nature of life as depicted by the life cycle of the lotus. First there is just an empty pond, since the lotus begins as a seed. It then becomes leaves, followed by the flower, and finally, at the end of its cycle, it goes back to being seed again; once more all we see is an empty pond. The *koan* also hints at the Zen idea that there is no beginning and no end – only "being." It also refers to the impermanent nature of our lives, for Zen regards everything in this world as being temporary. This idea is also found in the

*Heart Sutra*, a sacred Buddhist scripture, which says that all things recognized through the senses are nothing other than emptiness; and that emptiness is nothing other than all things seen through the senses. In Zen, to see the true nature of an object is to recognize the world beyond its appearance.

Many of the more conventional Buddhist teachings derived from the lotus are filled with hope and inspiration. For in its struggle to bring beauty and purity into the world, the lotus shows us how we can overcome delusions of the ego and avoid those things that cause suffering and misery to others. The lotus starts its journey in the depths of muddy ponds and marshes. Yet out of this darkness, there comes a blossom so pure and pristine that it overcomes all the imperfections of the world that it leaves behind. As the lotus flower awakens from the murky waters and pushes its way to the surface, its heart-shaped bud reaches up to the sunshine. This evocative shape is often likened to the Buddhist gesture of holding the hands together when greeting someone (known as *gassho*). Then slowly, in the warmth of the sun, the flower opens to reveal its full glory, making the world around it a more beautiful place.

This journey into the light is like the spiritual awakening of the heart. It is a reminder of the strength that lies within us all to overcome the problems of life and achieve perfection. The silvery pearls formed by raindrops that gather on the lotus's leaves are thought of as pearls of wisdom – there for all of us to learn from if we only took the time to look.

The lotus also shows us how we can set an example to those around us. In its journey to reach its goal, it causes no hurt or pain. Likewise, our thoughts, words or actions should not cause suffering to others. When our hearts blossom with pure thoughts, we radiate love and understanding. Like the lotus, our strength and presence will provide inspiration to those who face similar struggles.

# bamboo: the blessing from heaven

Of all the things in nature that have helped to shape Eastern philosophy, no plant has been venerated to quite the same degree as bamboo. For no plant – other than perhaps rice – has played such an essential role in the lives, culture and customs of literally billions of people throughout Asia.

To appreciate the role of bamboo in Zen, the influence of the ancient Chinese science of *feng shui* – the art of harmonious placement or ordering within a specific environment – must be considered. *Feng shui* evolved in early rural China when people's lives depended on the fertility of the earth, which in turn relied on plentiful sunshine and water. As people began to observe the patterns of nature more closely, they realized that the ideal harmony between heaven, earth and themselves hinged on the auspicious placement of their farms, houses or orchards. So they used *feng shui* – which involves balancing Yin and Yang energies – to determine where and how they should construct buildings and fashion the landscape. Thus, *feng shui* was used to enhance nature – not disturb it. And owing to its widespread presence in the natural landscape, bamboo played an important part in this attempt to create harmony. When, in early China, bamboo was planted in gardens or areas that surrounded houses and buildings sited through *feng shui*, it was thought to allow favorable *ch'i* energy to circulate around the property and to create the sought-after rhythm and order of a natural landscape.

Across Asia, bamboo is regarded as both beautiful and practical – as a "blessing from heaven" – and is still widely used as a building material and for a vast range of domestic furniture, tools and other items. However, it is not just cherished for its beauty and usefulness. Throughout China, Japan and other parts of Asia, bamboo symbolizes many different virtues or qualities, such as fidelity, wisdom and longevity. In China, for example, it represents humility, modesty and eternal youth, as well as joy, laughter, peace, serenity and good fortune. It is also considered, along with the plum, the orchid and the chrysanthemum, to be one of the traditional "four noble plants" that symbolize happiness.

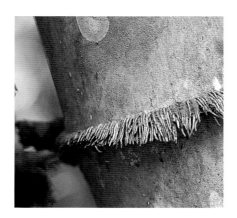

In Zen, bamboo is respected for its strength and resilience. It was also highly prized for its beauty and strong shape and was therefore planted in Zen temple landscape gardens and the Edo stroll gardens. From the very start, Zen scholars, writers and poets have admired both its strength and ability to bend but not yield in high winds. Because of these attributes, bamboo often features in Zen *koans* and paintings – especially the medieval Chinese-influenced ink-wash paintings created by Japanese Zen monks.

Bamboo's resilience and its bountiful supply make it an ideal material for fences, screens, trellises and gates, as well as for frames or canes to support other plants, in Zen and other Asian gardens. Many early Chinese gardens had a high bamboo fence around them as protection against negative energy emanating from the house. Inside the fence, a basket made of matted bamboo leaves was placed on a long pole and raised over the garden wall to ward off this harmful *sha* energy from the property and bring good fortune to the occupants.

Bamboo was introduced by the early Zen gardeners to the temple gardens of Kyoto not only because of its symbolism but also because of its color and architectural appearance. Tall, dark green canes of bamboo were used in gardens like Tenryu-ji to create a feeling of *yugen* as well as to contrast with the vivid colors of the deciduous trees in autumn. The bamboo in these Zen temple gardens grows to heights of over 10m (30ft) and creates a dramatic feature on the hillsides and along the paths that lead to shrines or smaller temples. In Kamakura the bamboo temple, known as Hokoku-ji, is a small Zen Rinzai temple dedicated to bamboo and it houses the grave of an important member of the Ashikaga family. Here the bamboo is known as *moshu* and was originally transplanted from Kyoto. It is highly prized for its appearance and over the years it has been the inspiration for many Zen poems and observations.

Finally, besides being the provider of brushes, paper and writing tablets for Chinese and Japanese calligraphers, bamboo is also a source of food as well as a fount of artistic and spiritual inspiration.

禅道

# the ways of zen

Bow down
to the Buddha –
master of the artless art

# the ways of zen

Because of the sheer size of China and the diversity of its people it is difficult to assess fully the impact of Zen Buddhism on Chinese culture. Certainly during the Sung Dynasty (1121–1279), Zen or Ch'an was one of the most powerful spiritual influences in the development of Chinese culture and had a lasting influence on all the arts – particularly on calligraphy, poetry and ink-wash painting. Chinese Zen monasteries became centers for classical studies as well as philosophical, scholarly and artistic pursuits.

In Japan, however, matters were very different. Over the course of time, Zen had a more profound influence on the culture of Japan than it ever had on the country of its birth. From the thirteenth century onward, Zen monks traveled to China and returned with highly prized paintings, poetry, ceramics and furnishings. Japanese culture soon began to assimilate these Zen-inspired Chinese art forms – with the result that in Japan art and religion became closely entwined. In addition to Japan's architecture and landscape gardening, Zen influenced nearly every aspect of daily life, from drinking tea and arranging flowers to calligraphy and painting. Many consider Japanese haiku – a form of Zen poetry still highly regarded for its eloquence and verbal economy – to embody the essence of Zen. Sung-inspired traditional ink-wash artworks (*sumi-e*) flourished in the fourteenth and fifteenth centuries and were often painted by Zen monks, who imitated the landscape images of China, using them as metaphorical expressions of Zen. With their creative use of white space they could express hidden depth and suggest cosmic principles.

Both the creative and martial arts in Japan flourished under the influence of Zen. As scholars, artists and samurai alike sought to express a deeper understanding of Zen's profound philosophy, their endeavors gave rise to a number of new disciplines that have become known as "the ways of zen." Although often esoteric in their execution, these various art forms set out to show an appreciation of everyday things and to celebrate nature itself. Everything in the world surrounding

the Zen scholar was seen as having a deeper inner truth – its Buddha-nature – and so could point the way to enlightenment.

By the time of the Edo period (1603–1866), each of these specific Zen-related practices became known as a "way" or *dō*, giving rise to such martial arts terms as aikido (the way of self defence), *kyudō* (the way of the bow) and kendo (the way of the sword). Likewise, the various Zen art forms such as *kadō* (the way of the flower), *chadō* or *sadō* (the way of tea) and *shodō* (the way of writing) all originate from these traditions and teachings of Zen.

With all these art forms, what was more important than mastering their basic principles or techniques was to become one with their spiritual aspects. It is in this "inner" approach that the real significance of the specific discipline lies – not just in the final attainment of a work of art or a new skill. This state of mind, known as *munen* or *muso* – "no thought, no reflection" – involves letting your natural ability act in a consciousness-free form, unburdened by thoughts, deliberation or partiality of any kind.

Many Zen ink-wash paintings of the Muromachi period were felt to embody the very essence of the Zen approach to art. The inner meaning of a painting was compared to enlightenment – artistic inspiration sprang from the depths of one's inner consciousness and so this art epitomized the Zen attitude to reality. For ultimately, all the ways of Zen lead to a deeper understanding of the harmony of form and void and of the infinite beauty found in the silence of emptiness and space that their art expresses. They lead, in other words, to the very spirit of Zen itself.

# *chadō*: the way of tea

The Japanese have a unique ability to convert philosophy into art. Nowhere is this more evident than in the tea ceremony or *cha-no-yu*, which is designed to engender a frame of mind that will lead directly to the inner truth of Zen Buddhism. This "spirit of tea" embraces Zen's teachings on transcendentalism and emptiness and also stems from earlier, Taoist-inspired aesthetics of naturalism and simplicity.

The origins of the tea ceremony itself go back to the ancient Chinese Zen Buddhist monasteries, where tea was used as a medicine and also as a stimulant to stay awake while praying and meditating. Tea drinking was then brought to Japan by the first Japanese Zen monks and soon became an inseparable part of temple life. Under the guidance of the first tea masters of the Momoyama period such as Sen-no-Rikyu (1521–1591), the art of tea drinking was essentially transformed to induce a higher state of consciousness. Instead of taking place among showy possessions and finery in the large palatial tea rooms of Muromachi times, tea drinking was brought back to a simpler spiritual ritual known as *wabi cha* and was performed in a rustic teahouse (*soan*) that simulated a scholarly hermit's hut in a remote retreat. Influenced by the aesthetics of naturalism and *wabi sabi* and by the desire for solitude and escape from the pressures of the outside world, the tea ceremony became a means of finding solace and sanctuary in a natural setting.

The way of tea has had a profound and far-reaching effect on the culture of Japan. The tea ceremony itself in its pure form is an almost solemn ritual acted out between host and guests. It has a set of procedures, movements and etiquette that are all performed at a measured, tranquil pace to allow time for reflection and contemplation. It is in essence an exercise in aesthetics that teaches many of the virtues that were central to both Taoist and early Zen philosophy. At the core of *chadō* are four basic concepts that summarize the disciplines of tea: *wa* (harmony); *kei* (respect); *sei* (purity); and *jaku* (tranquillity).

Words

from the brush –

pictures in the mind

# *shodō*: the way of writing

As long ago as the fifth century c.e., the Japanese adopted Chinese pictogram word characters known as *kanji*. Over time they refined them and created their own characters known as *kana*. Today Japanese artists still use both *kanji* and *kana* characters in their work. By the Heian period (794–1185), calligraphy using *kanji* had become an established art form in Japan, which meant that medieval Japanese Zen scholars were able to understand and translate the works of the great Chinese calligraphers, painters, poets and writers of the Sung dynasty. Because of their high regard for these Chinese artists, Zen monks began copying their scrolls and artworks and, as with Chinese scholars of the time, placed considerable emphasis on the style and quality of their calligraphy. Their endeavors led to the Zen-inspired art form of *shodō* – the way of writing or calligraphy using a brush.

From the start of the Ashikaga shogunate and the re-establishment of Kyoto as the country's capital in 1333, traditional Zen-inspired ink-wash painting became the fashion as Japanese masters began to popularize the style of the Chinese Sung painters. It was customary for artists to adorn these paintings not only with their signatures but also with a description or a poignant poem that related to the subject matter. They would do this with a brush in *kanji* characters, which soon became an integral part of the artwork. In addition, many Sung scrolls of calligraphy containing Chinese poems or profound sayings were imported to Japan – again inspiring Japanese artists to produce similar works. These *shodō* scrolls – known as *kakemono* or sometimes *kakejiku* – are highly treasured and much admired. To this day they are hung in Zen temples as well as teahouse alcoves.

*Shodō* by its very nature is a highly skilled technique that has become so developed that the creation of characters virtually owes more to art than to writing. It requires a deep understanding of how to work within empty spaces to express "the content of the void" – an image of the unseen. To learn this marriage of emptiness and form requires considerable training and instruction even to grasp the basic skills and to adopt the right Zen frame of mind and spiritual approach for its correct execution.

# *kadō*: the way of flowers

Flower arranging in Japan has developed into a serious art form practiced by both men and women, often as an extension of *cha-no-yu*, the tea ceremony. By its very method it expresses the unity in Zen between art and nature. This disciplined yet beautiful and natural form of arranging flowers is known as *ikebana*. *Kadō* itself refers to the "way of flowers" as a whole – as well as to the deeper meanings found in the spirit of this ancient art, which has arisen from the Japanese people's intimate relationship with the natural world. Learning the way of flowers requires years of instruction from a recognized master, not only to grasp the technique but to understand the meaning and symbolism linked to the teachings of Zen. Art is studied in Japan not just for art's sake but for spiritual gain and insight as part of the search for the "real truth." All the ways of Zen have two aspects to them: a significant metaphysical side as well as a practical side. In *kadō* the skillful dexterity needed to arrange flowers becomes a form of meditation in itself.

The religious origins of *kadō* can be traced back to the Buddhist temples of China, where flowers were placed in heavy bronze vessels filled with sand and placed before the image of the Buddha. By medieval times, as Zen developed in Japan, simpler, more eloquent flower arrangements were devised that suited the austere style of Zen temples. However, the real tradition of *kadō* has been consciously shaped by Japan's tea cult and the guiding aesthetics that surround *cha-no-yu*.

The refinements and sensitivities of this art form were essentially developed to suit the design and character of the teahouse. Simple, natural flower arrangements were created to be placed in the alcove or *tokonoma* of the teahouse, where they could be appreciated by guests and play their role in the ritual and rhythm of the tea ceremony.

Today, flower arranging in Japan has become a secular art. But the true *kadō* leads to the release of all one's full creative powers and requires an inner discipline and self-denial that comes only from the Zen mind and spirit.

# *koh-dō*: the way of incense

Virtually unknown in the West, the traditional Japanese art of *koh-dō*, the way of incense, has, like the tea ceremony and other Zen expressions, developed its own traditions and principles. Once used by the samurai to sharpen their senses before going into battle, *koh-dō* has also developed into a guessing game in which participants try to identify the fragrances of different incense.

The use of incense in everyday life goes back to ancient India, where exotic woods were burned as a perfume for clothing and rooms. The idea of using incense reached Japan in the sixth century; and by the fourteenth century the samurai class had developed the way of *koh* as an element of *bushidō*, the way of the warrior. Incense reached the height of its popularity in the seventeenth century during the Edo period, when burning it became a popular pastime among all classes of the population. There are now different schools of *koh-dō*: the two main ones are the Oiye-ryu, founded by the aristocrats of the Imperial family; and the Shino-ryu, founded by members of the samurai class.

The various woods used in the making of incense or *kohboku* mainly come from Southeast Asia. The Japanese have prized them throughout their history and have used them as tokens of loyalty to their lords or rulers. Also, because of the woods' great value, *kohboku* itself has often been valued as a symbol of power and authority.

Apart from finding sensual pleasure in the fragrance of incense, practitioners of the way of *koh* can gain a profound satisfaction from the ritual's aesthetic beauty and spiritual depth. *Koh-dō* can be performed either in a group or individually. It inspires a Zen-like mood of calm and quiet reflection in a busy world.

Incense has always played an important part in Zen Buddhism. Used as an offering of purification, it also plays an essential role in religious ceremonies and rituals. Even today, large incense burners are located at the entrance to many Zen temples; and incense is burned on the altars or in front of images of the Buddha.

In all the universe

there is but

one truth

# the infinite unity of the universe

As the boundaries of science rapidly expand and our awareness about the environment increases, we face the fact that an ecological disaster of man's making is a very real threat to the human race and all life on earth. Man's avarice and ignorance are destroying our planet at an alarming rate. The environment is being polluted. The earth's resources are rapidly being depleted. Every year, whole forests and millions of trees are being destroyed. Many species and their habitats are threatened or have become extinct.

Through living Zen, we realize that our lives are intrinsically linked with the environmental ethic of this earth. Practicing Zen means studying the self as well as living in harmony with nature's inherent order. Zen Buddhism teaches that all life is interconnected: it requires us to take responsibility for our own lives and for all living things. We are all part of an infinite net that attaches each of us to every living organism and element in the universe. Nothing separates us – we are but a single entity. All living things are interrelated, from the smallest atom to the greatest sun in the cosmos. Everything needs everything else. We all pulse as one great heartbeat – what affects our world also impacts on the farthest star in the heavens. The universe is one, and every flower, leaf, insect, animal, person or planet is part of its infinite unity. To understand this primordial belief is to make a major leap forward in our perception of reality: when we accept this idea of "interconnectedness" eventually all duality disappears. When this extraordinary realization hits home we can begin to see the "self" not with the separateness that has been part of our lifetime's conditioning but in a totally holistic way that causes us to relate to the universe with care and responsiveness. For how we see the self is how we see the universe.

This wisdom should not be wasted. Living Zen empowers us to cherish and care for the environment. Once we become aware that own bodies and minds and the universe are one and the same we must take responsibility not only for our own lives but also for this earth. For Zen has revealed to us one of the great mysteries of life. It has opened our eyes and shown that both the universe and our lives have no boundaries – no outside – no end.

# picture captions

**1** Horse chestnut in bud.
**2** The path in the Zen garden symbolizes "the way" and represents the passage of man in his life on earth.
**6–7** Sunset over Mt Fuji from Shonan Beach in Japan.
**8** A dried Japanese maple leaf.
**9** A bamboo waterspout (*kakei*) used for washing in a Zen tea garden.
**10** A lotus in bud. The flower is considered sacred in Buddhism.
**11** The style and design of this 300-year-old tea bowl was influenced by the famous tea master Sen-no-Rikyu.
**12** The roof garden at Kahitsu-kan, The Kyoto Museum of Contemporary Art, Japan.
**13** Carefully stored teacups in a Zen-style kitchen.
**14–15** A typical Zen flower arrangement with rosehips silhouetted in front of a *shoji* screen.
**16** Daibutsu, the great stone buddha in Kamakura, Japan, was made in 1252 and is nearly 12m (37ft) in height.
**17** Burning incense – a means of purification in Zen rituals and liturgy.
**18** Fallen leaves on the damp cobblestones of a Zen temple's steps.
**19** A Buddhist temple gate in all its autumn splendor in Anraku-ji, Kyoto.
**20** The head of the famous buddha, Jizo-bosatsu, at the Kencho-ji Zen temple in Kamakura.
**21** Religious objects used in Zen temple ceremonies. *Above*: An incense burner. *Center*: A drum (*ohdaiko*). *Below*: An abbot's chair.
**22** First light in the mountains – early Chinese and Japanese landscape paintings tried to capture this feeling of "nothingness."
**23** Incense burning at the entrance to the Kencho-ji Zen temple in Kamakura.
**24** The early morning mists of autumn in Arashi-yama, Kyoto.
**25** The Lake District in England – reflections of reeds in the calm waters of a lake.
**26** Ancient Chinese characters carved in wood meaning *hinpotsu*, the literal translation of which is "A declaration of a Zen abbot's spiritual break through to enlightenment." This tablet hangs in the Buddha hall at the Kencho-ji Zen temple in Kamakura.
**27** Jizo-bosatsu, the main buddha at the Zen Rinzai sect temple of Kencho-ji.
**28** Bonsho, the famous temple bell at the Kencho-ji Zen temple, is a national treasure in Japan.
**29** Zen temple artefacts. *Above*: An altar incense burner. *Center*: *Moku-gyo*, a hollow instrument for beating time to religious chants. *Below*: A statue of an ancient Zen master in the Buddha hall at the Kencho-ji Zen temple.
**30** The Japanese *kanji* character, meaning emptiness or sky, carved into a wooden chest.
**31** Japanese maple trees in autumn at the Tenryu-ji Zen temple in Kyoto.
**32–33** An autumn dawn at Arashi-yama. A pine hangs over the still waters of the river.
**34** Symbolic kaki fruit or persimmons growing by the lake at the famous Zen temple of Roan-ji in Kyoto.
**35** *Above*: A set of *teppatsu* bowls, which are used by Zen Buddhist monks to hold food given to them by lay persons on their alms round

(*takuhatsu*). *Center*: Leaves on the mossy ground at the Saiho-ji moss temple in Kyoto. *Below*: The shrine gate at the Tenryu-ji Zen temple in Kyoto.
**36** A white water lily after a heavy rain storm.
**37** A sprig of pine.
**38** *Above*: A snail. *Center*: An unfurling fern. *Below*: Moss-covered steps.
**39** A valuable Chinese Imperial celadon-glazed tea bowl.
**40–41** Carp have long been a popular motif and religious symbol in Chinese and Japanese Zen art.
**42** *Teppatsu* bowls, which are used today to serve Zen temple vegetarian dishes known as *shojin ryori,* or food for practice.
**43** Raking the Zen garden not only serves a practical purpose, it is also a form of meditation.
**44** Pebbles in a modern Zen garden.
**45** A *chōzubachi* or water bowl – a symbol of spiritual purification found in Zen tea gardens.
**46** *Zōri* (straw sandals) worn by Zen monks.
**47** A Buddhist monk making the sign of *gassho* – an action of deep respect and gratitude for the teaching – in front of an image of Buddha.
**48** A mossy Zen temple path in Kyoto.
**49** Cherry blossom.
**50** An alcove (*tokonoma*) cut into a plain wall.
**51** People often burn a candle while meditating.
**52–53** A monk sitting in contemplation.
**54** The interior of a *zendo* or meditation hall in a Zen temple.
**55** The wall of a *zendo*.
**56** An outside bath (*roten-buro*) at a mountain hot spring (*onsen*).
**57** A place to sit in contemplation at Huka Lodge in New Zealand.
**58–59** Zen temple cooking (*shojin ryori*).
**60** A stream with carp in a Zen garden in Tenryu-ji, Kyoto.
**61** Fuji-san, the inspiration for many Zen poems, is the sacred mountain of Japan.
**62–63** The Tokyo International Forum building, designed by Raphael Viniori.
**64** Yasaka-no-tō, the Chinese pagoda-style temple in the Gion area of Kyoto.
**65** A mythical Chinese phoenix bird sits on top of the spire of this *kara-yo* (Chinese style) religious building in the Gion area of Kyoto.
**66** Examples of *kara-yo* (Chinese style) Zen temple architecture.
**67** A Chinese-influenced *hojo* or abbot's quarters, with its principal gate opening onto the *kare-san-sui* (artificial) garden at the Tofuku-ji Zen temple in Kyoto.
**68** A Chinese-influenced ink-wash screen painting (c. 1550), showing a scholar's retreat in some remote region with high mountains and deep valleys. The screen hangs in the Ryogen-in Zen temple, Daitoku-ji, Kyoto.
**69** Various woods used for the floors, shutters and walls of old Zen temples.
**70** The Silver Pavilion or Kannonden, at the Ginkaku-ji Zen temple in Kyoto. It was built by the famous shogun Yoshimasa Ashikaga in 1482.
**71** The interior of a rustic Japanese teahouse (*soan*) showing a flower arrangement and *shoji* screens.
**72** A room in the *hojo* at the Ryogen-in Zen temple.
**73** The austere interior of the *zendo* at the Kencho-ji Zen temple in Kamakura.
**74** A modern alcove (*tokonoma*) in Senju-an

Ryokan (a traditional Japanese country retreat), Gunma prefecture, Japan.
**75** *Shoji* screens.
**76** Contemporary architecture and design clearly influenced by Zen aesthetics.
**77** The Zen-inspired architecture of St. Mary's Cathedral in Gokoku-ji, Tokyo, designed by the Japanese architect Tange.
**78** Examples of Zen architecture.
**79** The entrance hall of the Tepia building in the Aoyama district of Tokyo, designed by the architect Fumihiko Maki.
**80–81** The reception room at the Hempel hotel, London.
**82–83** Zen interiors in Senju-an Ryokan, Gunma prefecture, Japan.
**84** Various Zen-influenced interiors.
**85** The light-filled interiors of the Hempel, London.
**86** Furniture in the Zen interior is simple, well designed and aesthetically pleasing.
**87** The Hempel, London.
**88–89** The Japanese tradition of using natural materials is central to the Zen living space.
**90–91** A Zen-inspired interior in a loft apartment, London.
**92** A *tokonoma* – a type of alcove used for displaying works of art and simple flower arrangements – in the Zen temple at Daitoku-ji, Kyoto.
**93** Examples of tatami – woven straw mats that are an ingredient of the traditional Japanese interior.
**94–95** Zen-influenced interiors in a loft-style apartment, London.
**96–97** Light diffused through *shoji* screens adds to the spirituality of the traditional Zen interior.
**98** A meditation space in a traditional Japanese house.
**99** The clean, unadorned spaces in a Zen home inspire free-flowing thoughts.
**100** The classic shapes of plain white bowls are displayed in the corridors of The Hempel, London.
**101** Wooden bowls by Babylon Design.
**102–3** In the Zen home only a few objects are displayed so their beauty can be fully appreciated.
**104–5** The famous Zen moss garden of Ryogintei at the Ryogen-in Zen temple in Daitioku-ji, Kyoto. Created by the artist Soami in the Muromachi period, the main stone represents Mt Shumisen, the sacred Buddhist mountain that is thought to be the core of the universe.
**106** Morning mist over the Zen landscape gardens of Tenryu-ji in Kyoto.
**107** Wet rice fields have changed the landscape around this old Japanese village.
**108** Zen gardens were designed to express a deeper understanding of Zen principles.
**109** In Zen gardens stone bridges (*bashi*) symbolized the linking of two worlds.
**110–11** Isshidan, the famous Zen *kare-san-sui* garden in Ryogen-in, Kyoto. The central island represents a sea turtle and the main rock at the back, Mt Horai in China.
**112** Rocks have always played a symbolic role in the Zen garden.
**113** Totekiko, the small *kare-san-sui* garden of the Ryogen-in Zen temple in Kyoto. It depicts the powerful ripples spreading out from a stone thrown into water.
**114** The famous Zen rock garden of Ryoan-ji in Kyoto.

**115** Raked patterns of sand in Zen *kare-san-sui* gardens represent waves, ripples or the flow of water.
**116–17** In symbolic Zen landscapes, designers set out to imitate the scenes from Chinese landscape ink-wash paintings.
**118** A *tsukubai* tea garden – a collection of stones mainly making up a water basin (*chozubachi*) used for purifying the hands and mouth prior to the tea ceremony.
**119** Scenes from the tea garden. *Above*: The waiting bench (*koshikake machiai*). *Center*: The middle gate (*chu-mon*). *Below*: A stepping stone (*tobi-ishi*).
**120** A tea garden. *Above*: *Roji*, the dewy path to the teahouse. *Center*: High wooden sandals (*geta*) used for walking in the tea garden. *Below*: Stepping stones (*tobi-ishi*).
**121** A *sekimori-ishi* – a stone wrapped with black string, which indicates no entry beyond that point.
**122–23** Features of the tea garden: water basins (*chozubachi*), lanterns (*ishidōrō*), yellow flowers (*tsuwabuki*) and moss-covered stepping stones (*tobi-ishi*).
**124** The *ichimatsu* patterned moss garden at the Tofuku-ji Zen temple in Kyoto.
**125** Details from Zen moss gardens in Kyoto.
**126–27** Water plays a central role in modern Zen gardens in Auckland, New Zealand.
**128–29** Simplicity and a focus on clean lines

and shapes are the secrets of the modern Zen garden.
**130** A naturally shaped rock forms the base for a pillar in a modern Zen garden in Bali.
**131** A modern interpretation of the Zen *kare-san-sui* garden using hard landscaping techniques. The garden belongs to the Tepia building in the Aoyama district of Tokyo.
**132** A lotus flower.
**133–34** The leaf of the lotus also has great importance in Buddhist beliefs.
**135** The life cycle of the lotus flower from bud to seed pod.
**136** Yellow bamboo in Bali.
**137** This tall green bamboo, known as *mosodake*, is cultivated at Hōkoku-ji, the Zen bamboo temple in Kamakura.
**138–39** Bamboo is planted in Zen gardens for its color, architectural qualities and spiritual symbolism.
**140–41** The skilled *shodō* master's tools, used in the creation of the age-old Zen discipline of calligraphy.
**142** Priceless *shodō* brushes made from antique bamboo or cedar and the fur of deer or wild sable.
**143** Powdered green tea, known as *maccha*, used in the Japanese tea ceremony.
**144** The ways of Zen. *Above* and *below*: Objects used in *koh-dō* – the way of incense. *Center*: *Kadō* – the way of flowers.

**145** A black bamboo tea whisk (*chasen*) used for preparing tea in the tea ceremony (*cha-no-yu*).
**146** In the Japanese tea ceremony, special green tea (*maccha*) is prepared in a highly prized ceramic tea bowl.
**147** *Above*: A finely detailed *natsume* tea caddy used for storing powdered green tea. *Center*: A kettle (*tetsubim*) used for boiling water on a charcoal stove. *Below*: An unusually decorated ceramic tea bowl (*chawan*).
**148** An antique Chinese *suzuri* used for making the black ink for *shodō*.
**149** A *shodō* master practises the ancient Zen art of calligraphy.
**150–51** Zen flower arrangements.
**152** *Above*: An old scroll painting of Japanese noblemen practising *koh-dō*. *Center*: Wooden cards used to identify various fragrances. *Below*: An incense burner (*censer*) used for impregnating clothes with fragrance.
**153** The specialized instruments used in *koh-dō* for guessing the fragrance of various incense.
**154–55** The sun sets over the sea of Japan.
**156** High in the mountains of Japan the snow lies heavily on the trees.
**157** Wood anemones in spring.

---

# index

# author's acknowledgments

My sincerest thanks to . . . where do I start? So many people have been unbelievably kind and supportive! How can I begin to thank every one of you for all you did to help me? I only hope that for those of you whom I unfortunately miss out, when you read this book you will understand that my words, photographs and poetry are in themselves a profound token of my gratitude to all the special people of this world.

Starting in Japan I want to send a huge thank you to Hitoshi Ochiai – without his support and generosity this book would not have been completed. I also want to express my deepest gratitude to Yōko Murata, whose beautiful *shodō* has given this book a special quality. Mahoko Kiriyama's connections were invaluable! Thanks to Jiun Akamatsu for being a great model and friend as well as introducing me to the amazing Tōkō Nakamura, a man who has truly found the truth, an enlightened human being. He helped me so much and yet expected nothing in return. Without Tōkōsan's help I would have struggled to find such beautiful images. Thanks to Nakao Kenji, whose kindness and help were the deeds of a true gentleman, and to Yachiyo Yoshida, who fed us with care and compassion while in Kyoto.

In Tokyo I particularly want to thank the outstanding architect Takao Habuka, who showed us so much warmth, hospitality and kindness: *domo arigato gozaimas*. In Kamakura special thanks must go to the eminent Roshi Shōdō Yoshida, head abbot of Kencho-ji Zen temple, who allowed me to photograph in the Buddha hall. Also in Kyoto my deepest thanks and respect go to Shōdō Maeda-san, the *jushoku* (head Zen priest) at Zuihō-in, Daitoku-ji, for his generosity and good humor. The tea ceremony was a special occasion! A big thank you to the charming and welcoming Bunyo Azuma-san, the *jushoku* of Ryogen-in in the Daitoku-ji Zen temple. My very special thanks go to Mr. and Mrs. Fujimoto of Saiun-dō, who let me photograph their beautiful *shodō* materials, and the handsome Mr. Fujimoto, who kindly agreed to model for the book. Thanks to Sunagawa-san of Nakanishi-Taiheidō for letting me photograph his priceless tea ceremony objects and to Mr. Akinaga and Mr. Nakamura of Kungyoku-dō for helping with the *koh-dō* photographs. In Daitokuji

my thanks go to Atsushi Muto of the Izusen Shōjin restaurant and to Mr. Y. Terai for letting me photograph his beautiful tea garden called U-an – a unique experience! I should also mention the charming Haruka Satoh and her husband, along with the owner of the most beautiful *ryokan* (Japanese country retreat), Tawaraya in Kyoto, Mrs. Toshi Satoh. Finally, thank you to Kahitsu-kan, Museum of Contemporary Art in Kyoto, for letting me photograph their roof garden.

In London I would like to thank the following: at Colourworks – Paul Cornish, Colin Burgoyne and Brian East; at the Pro-Centre – Alistair and Kier for the loan of lots of gear; the guys at Metro Imaging, Chelsea, especially Paul and Clive; Christine Wilson and Robert Elms for letting me photograph their house; very special thanks to Alastair Hendy and his partner, John, for letting me use the photographs of their beautiful home in this book; to Henry Chebaane of the Hempel; to my dear friend Nobuyoshi Hamanaka at Kara Kara in South Kensington; and to Inge Cordsen at Livingstone Studios, Hampstead.

In New Zealand I must thank Jenny Gibbs for letting me photograph her outstanding garden; my dear friends Andrew and Heather Mackintosh for giving me spiritual nourishment and shelter so many times; and the talented architect Ron Sang. In Bali, many thanks to Michael White (Made Wijaya) and Linda Garland who shares my love of bamboo.

I also wish to express my deepest thanks to everyone at Frances Lincoln who made this book possible: especially Cathy Fischgrund for her vision and wisdom; Sarah Slack for her inspired design; Ginny Surtees for finishing the job; and James Harpur for his pragmatic and intelligent editing of my text.

And finally my special love and gratitude goes to my brother Anthony for teaching me so many things about gardens and the natural world.